WordPress for Beginners 2022

A Visual Step-by-Step Guide to Mastering WordPress

Updated 14th December 2021

"I work in the education department at one of the top academic institutions in the U.S., and if I could hire Dr. Williams to write all of my online training, I wouldn't hesitate." Laura

What people are saying about previous versions of this book:

"I work in the education department at one of the top academic institutions in the U.S., and if I could hire Dr. Williams to write all of my online training, I wouldn't hesitate..." **Laurie**

"This book is absolutely brilliant, and thanks to the author, I am about to go live with my new website. I had a great (in my opinion) idea for a website, I bought the domain for a WP hosted site but could not get my head around how to set it all up. The 'dummies' book for this (they are usually very good) made me feel like a..well, a dummy, to be honest, and assumed some prior knowledge. This didn't and took me step-by-step through everything. I worked my way diligently through it, chapter by chapter, as I put my site together. It's clearly set out, using a good size font (never underestimate the pleasure of a large font for a technical book!), the images were clear, and it was very easy to follow. He uses straightforward language, so it's like having a friend (the one who's patient and doesn't grit their teeth when you ask them to explain something for the third time) talk you through it. If you know absolutely nothing about WordPress but want to create a website, this is the book for you and the only one you will need." **Carole**

"If you take your time and read this book and act on all or even most of Andy's suggestions, you will not only have a much better understanding of WordPress you will also have a much-improved site." **Thomas**

"I can't praise this book enough, firstly because it shows everything on screen so clearly. I can have it open on my Kindle beside me and actually follow everything in WordPress on the computer. Also, It doesn't assume knowledge, and even I can follow the text. It takes a lot of talent as a technical writer to be able to put yourself in the shoes of someone who needs everything explaining. I am so glad I found this book. My blog will be up and running very soon." **Kindle Customer**

"Definitely the go-to guide! Since WordPress is a pretty easy format to get started on, I was able to make some progress. Then I found WordPress for Beginners, and WOW - my progress took off. Having a visual guide with extensive photos really helps those of us who are visual learners. But the best thing to me is that Williams not only describes what to do and how to do it, he explains why you should do it. I'm not a professional tech person, and this book is exactly what I needed. I suspect I will continue to refer to it in the future. Highly recommended." **Amazon Customer**

"Nailed It. I have been trying to install a working blog from time to time for the last four years, and of course, have read various books on the subject. It always got more complicated, with dashboards, PHP, SQL, SEO, or a shared WordPress site. This is the one book that does it flawlessly, and the installation actually works just as shown. The screenshots are accurate and most helpful as you step through each learning segment. Having written several technical

how-to manuals myself, I recognize a remarkably well structured and logical sequence of easy to learn, bite-sized topics." **Terry O'Hara**

"If you want to have a website but don't know-how, this book by Dr. Andy Williams will take you by the hand and walk you through the process of setting up your own blog correctly. He tells you not only exactly how to do it but also explains why you are taking the steps he walks you through. The instructions and visuals are clear and easy for anyone to follow." **J. Tanner**

"I Would Give This Book a 5 Plus. I literally started at page one and built my website from scratch without any prior experience because of this book. It was very easy to read and was laid out in a very logical, step by step order. I would recommend it without hesitation. I was so impressed with this book that I went and ordered several other of the author's books relating to developing an online presence." **GP**

"Clear, practical, and very helpful, WordPress for Beginners takes the reader step by step through the essentials of organizing your online world. Dr. Williams is a great writer and an excellent teacher. Highly recommended!" **Dr. James A. Holmund**

"Great lessons from a great teacher. Andy Williams really has a knack for organizing information in a clear, concise, and to-the-point manner. It is only a matter of following his excellent advice, and you will have a functioning WordPress site up and running in no time." **Prufrock**

"Why can't all guides be like this?" **B J Burton**

"Exemplary teaching. This book is a model of good teaching. Clear, uncluttered, direct. It takes you through the process with admirable clarity. I bought a printed guide to Word Press for twice the price, which left me utterly confused - this book should be used as an example of how to teach. Very highly recommended." **Amazon Customer**

"An excellent book. I logged into my account and just followed the book page by page, and in no time at all, I had a Website mapped out and running. The book is easy to follow, and you very quickly learn how WordPress works and how it can be used for writing Blogs, conventional Websites, and even combined ones if you are so inclined. This really is an excellent book to have in your programming library and is of great value in helping to steer through the morass of misinformation about WordPress on the web. I have just ordered the paperback version to have by my side, which I anticipate will become well-worn into the future." **Dr. A F Gerrard**

"Quite simply the best advice I've found............ Having spent a number of months getting disheartened and frustrated, I bought this book as a last-ditch attempt to get my website going before having to pay someone to do it for me. Setting up a website is not something I'd ever done before, so I had no technical knowledge at all. Quite simply, this book is superb.

It was just like having the web developer sitting next to me at my desk, talking me through every little detail. He 'told me' what to ignore (explaining why as he did so), explained what we were doing and why at every step, and the pictures aligned to what was on my screen as I went along. Two days later, I had a website, and now I am actually changing the theme and altering things with confidence. I simply cannot rate this book highly enough. Thank you, Andy!" **Louise Burridge**

"Brilliant - all you need to know to get up and running." **S. J. Oswald**

"I had to design a website urgently and one I could manage myself. I'd read that to do this, I needed a web design programme that offered CMS, Content Control Management, and that WordPress was the best programme for the job. I was a complete beginner with no knowledge at all about website design. Before I came across Dr. Andy Williams's book, I'd bought two others and became overwhelmed by the complexity and the jargon.

If you want to design your own website, you don't need any other book than this. If you work through it carefully and methodically, you'll quickly learn all the technicalities involved and have the vocabulary to create a website that is visually arresting. The content, of course, is up to you.

Dr. Williams is a natural-born teacher with that special genius of being able to make a complex process easy and interesting to follow. The large-format book is a pleasure to use. It begins with the assumption that the reader knows nothing about WordPress, website hosting, registering, and costs. The easy to follow steps takes you through this process to the point where once your website is up and running, the reader can download WordPress, then get to work! Dr. Williams takes you through every aspect of the WordPress 'dashboard' (the programme's control panel), a place it is important to know well, and where the web designer will spend a lot of time. Once the reader is familiar with this, the design process starts, and Dr. Williams again leads the reader step by step through the website building process.

One of the many outstanding features of the book is the use of screenshots that show the reader what to do and where to do it; it's like using a print out of a video. Another indispensable feature is the "Tasks to Complete" sections found at the end of each major learning phase. The reader is given a list of tasks to work through, which consolidates what has been learned and offers a comprehensive revision structure that can be revisited as many times as necessary.

"WordPress for Beginners" is not just an outstanding book about WordPress; it is also a model of how this kind of "teaching at a distance" should be done. Dr. Williams has written several other books using the same teaching techniques, and we can only hope the list continues to grow." **Dr. Gerald Benedict**

Disclaimer and Terms of Use Agreement

The author and publisher of this eBook and the accompanying materials have used their best efforts in preparing this eBook. The author and publisher make no representation or warranties with respect to the accuracy, applicability, fitness, or completeness of the contents of this eBook. The information contained in this eBook is strictly for educational purposes. Therefore, if you wish to apply ideas contained in this eBook, you are taking full responsibility for your actions.

The author and publisher disclaim any warranties (express or implied), merchantability, or fitness for any particular purpose. The author and publisher shall in no event be held liable to any party for any direct, indirect, punitive, special, incidental or other consequential damages arising directly or indirectly from any use of this material, which is provided "as is," and without warranties.

The author and publisher do not warrant the performance, effectiveness, or applicability of any sites listed or linked to in this eBook.

All links are for information purposes only and are not warranted for content, accuracy, or any other implied or explicit purpose.

The author and publisher of this book are not in any way associated with Google.

Contents

A Little Bit of History

In the early days, websites were hand-built using a code called Hypertext Markup Language, or HTML for short. To create good-looking websites, you needed to be something of a geek. Tools like Macromedia Dreamweaver (now owned by Adobe) and Microsoft FrontPage (discontinued in 2006) were developed to reduce the learning curve associated with building an HTML website, but these tools were expensive.

In May 2003, Matt Mullenweg & Mike Little released a tool that would change the face of website building forever. They called it WordPress. I must admit I was a little reluctant to give up my copy of Dreamweaver, but in 2004 I started to experiment with the WordPress platform. At that time, WordPress was just starting to get interesting with the introduction of plugins. We'll look at those later in the book, but for now, just understand that plugins are an easy and pain-free way of adding great new functionality to your website without needing any programming skills.

Fast-forward to today, and WordPress is now the site-building tool of choice for many professionals and enthusiasts alike. Home businesses run by moms & dads, school kids running blogs about their favorite bands, large corporations, and everyone in between have all turned to WordPress. It's extremely powerful, flexible, produces very professional looking websites or blogs, is relatively easy to use, and perhaps best of all, it's free. Sure, there is a learning curve, but that is where I come in.

With years of experience teaching technical stuff in an easy-to-understand manner, I am going to take you by the hand and guide you as you construct your very own professional looking website or blog, even if you know absolutely nothing about how to go about this. The only thing you need to know is how to use a web browser. If you have ever searched Google for something, you already have the skills necessary to follow this book.

I have made this book a step-by-step, visual guide to creating your website. Just follow along with the exercises, and in no time at all, you'll be using WordPress like a pro. You'll build a website you can be proud to show your family and friends. They will probably start asking YOU to help them build their website.

Excited? OK, let's get on with it.

How to Use This Book

I do not recommend you just sit down and read this book. The problem is that a lot of this book describes processes you need to do on your computer. If you try to read without following along on your computer, you will get lost and not be too sure what I am talking about.

This book is a hands-on tutorial. To get the most out of it, I recommend that you sit at your computer with the book open in front of you and follow along as you work your way through.

I'll use screenshots in the book that best demonstrate the point. These may be from a couple of my real sites or a demo site installed on my computer.

Whenever I do something on my demo site, you should try it on your site. Don't be afraid of making mistakes; just have fun and experiment with WordPress. Mistakes can easily be undone or deleted, and anyway, most of us learn better by making a few blunders along the way.

By the end of this book, you will have a solid understanding of how WordPress works and how you can get it to do what YOU want it to do. If you decide to take your WordPress knowledge to the next level, you'll have an excellent foundation to build on.

Towards the end of the book is a chapter called "Building 3 Site Models." This section will highlight WordPress's flexibility as a site creation tool by showing you how to use WordPress to build a typical website, a business site, and a blog. I'll provide you with links to videos showing demo site builds for these three types of websites using WordPress. Use these videos together with the content of this book to design the type of site you want.

Updates & Changes to WordPress?

When this book was written, the current version of WordPress was 5.6. However, the WordPress ecosystem changes a lot, and while most of these changes will be minor (you may not even notice them), some bigger changes can happen. After this book is published, there isn't much I can do to notify you of these changes. Therefore, I have set up a page on my website for book owners so that updates, changes, and issues can be listed. If something in the book does not look right, visit the updates page here:

https://ezseonews.com/wp2022/

You can leave comments on that page if you need to.

A Note About UK v US English

There are some differences between UK and US English. While I try to be consistent, some errors may slip into my writing because I spend a lot of time corresponding with people in both the UK and the US. The line can blur.

Examples of this include the spelling of words like optimise (UK) v optimize (US).

The difference I get the most complaints about is with collective nouns. Collective nouns refer to a group of individuals, e.g., Google. In the US, collective nouns are singular, so **Google IS** a company. However, in the UK, collective nouns are usually plural, so **Google ARE** a company. This is not to be confused with Google, "the search engine," which is singular in both.

There are other differences too. I hope that if I have been inconsistent anywhere in this book, it does not detract from the value you get from it.

WordPress itself will have some differences depending on whether you are using UK or US English. The one I find most obvious is in the labeling of the area containing things you have deleted.

If you installed WordPress with US English, you'd see this called "trash":

But if your WordPress is installed with UK English, this becomes "bin":

There are other places in the dashboard that use localized words like this. I'll leave those for you to find.

Found Typos in This Book?

Errors can get through proof-readers, so if you do find any typos or grammatical errors in this book, I'd be very grateful if you could let me know using this email address:

typos@ezseonews.com

What is WordPress?

WordPress is a Content Management System (CMS). That just means it is a piece of software that can help you manage and organize your content into an impressive and coherent website.

WordPress was created as a blogging tool, but it has become so much more than that over the years. Today, many WordPress driven sites look nothing like blogs (unless that's what the user wants). This is down to the flexibility of this amazing tool.

WordPress powers simple blogs, corporate websites, and everything in between. Companies like Sony, the Wall Street Journal, Samsung, New York Times, Wired, CNN, Forbes, Reuters, and many others all use WordPress as part of their online presence.

WordPress is open-source software, meaning that all of its code is free to view, use, and customize. This has enabled programmers worldwide to create extensions to this powerful publishing platform, from website templates to plugins that extend this amazing site building tool's functionality.

Some of the Features That Make WordPress Great

• The template system for site design means that changing your site's look and feel is as simple as installing a new theme with just a few clicks of the mouse. There are a plethora of free and quality WordPress themes available.

• Plugins are pieces of code that you can download into your WordPress site to add new features and functions. There are tens of thousands of plugins available, and many are free.

• Once your site is set up, you can concentrate on adding great content to your site. You simply build your page in the WordPress Dashboard, hit publish, and WordPress takes care of the rest.

• WordPress has a feature called Widgets that allows the user to drag and drop "features" into their site. For example, you could add a visitor poll to your site's sidebar using a widget. Widgets are typically used in the sidebars and footers, but some templates allow widgets to be placed in other well-chosen areas of the design.

• WordPress can help you with the SEO (Search Engine Optimization) of your site so that it has the potential to rank higher in search engines like Google and Bing.

• WordPress can create just about any type of site, for example, a hobby blog, a business site, or an e-commerce store.

WordPress.com v WordPress.org

There is a largely unknown, yet vital fact, that many WordPress beginners don't know. Are you ready for this? OK, here goes...

There are two "flavors" of WordPress!

These are commonly referred to as WordPress.com and WordPress.org and you need to know the difference before you start building your site.

WordPress.com and WordPress.org refer to the website where that version of WordPress is available. If you visit those sites, you'll notice they are very different.

Here is the current wordpress.com homepage:

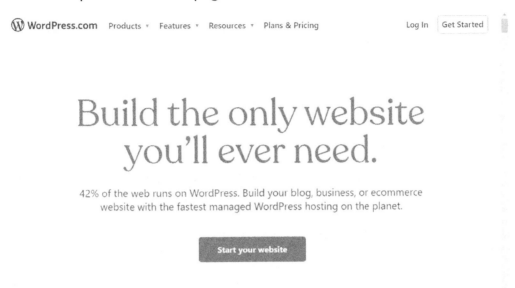

And the wordpress.org homepage:

Both of these versions of WordPress are from the same company, and use the same underlying WordPress code. But they target different user groups, so they look and behave a little differently.

With WordPres.com, WordPress the company are in control of everything, so you have to accept quite a lot of limitations in all but the most expensive subscription plan. With WordPress.org, you are in control and can do what you like, *at a fraction of the cost*.

You must understand the difference between these two so let's dig a little deeper.

WordPress.com

The good news with WordPress.com is that you can sign up and build a free website. WordPress.com hosts your site on their servers (computers).

For example, let's suppose you wanted to create a website on "educational toys for kids." You could set up a website called educationaltoysforkids.wordpress.com (assuming no one else has already taken that name).

Your website address (URL) would be:

educationaltoysforkids.wordpress.com

By visiting that address in your web browser, you'd see the homepage of your site.

You'll notice that your website URL includes ".wordpress.com" on the end of it. Your site domain is known as a sub-domain of the wordpress.com.

There are paid ways to use an actual domain, like educationaltoysforkids.com which looks much better,

The main downside is that you do not own the site; WordPress.com does. One day you might go to look at your site and find that it's no longer there. You are playing by their rules.

There are also restrictions on WordPress.com. For example, you won't be able to install any plugin you like, and you'll have a limited choice of themes (skins to change the way your site looks). You cannot show any adverts on your site either, though WordPress.com can insert its adverts into your pages. The free WordPress.com is, therefore, only useful for non-profit websites.

Note that some paid plans lift some of the free account restrictions, but these work out more expensive when compared like-for-like with a WordPress.org website. For example, you can remove WordPress.com adverts for $4 per month. However, to remove WordPress.com branding, get access to themes of your choice, and install any plugin you want, you'd need a Business subscription, which currently costs $25 per month. By comparison, using wordpress.org requires a web host costing as little as $2.95 a month, and you don't have any limitations.

The interface (Dashboard) on WordPress.com websites is also greatly simplified and completely different from the one you'll get with the full-blown WordPress.org.

For these reasons, I do not recommend you create your site on WordPress.com.

If you are drawn to WordPress.com because there is a free option and don't want to buy a domain and hosting while you learn to use WordPress, there is another option. Install the full-blown WordPress.org on your computer!

How to do this is beyond the scope of this book, but you will find tutorials on my website. Check the resources at the end of this book for a link. Once on my site, search for "local install."

Whatever you decide, this book will assume you are using WordPress from WordPress.org.

Do you still want to use WordPress.com?

After everything I have said, if you still want to use WordPress.com and follow this book, you can. Just be aware of the differences, including those in the dashboard.

Here is what the default dashboard looks like at WordPress.com:

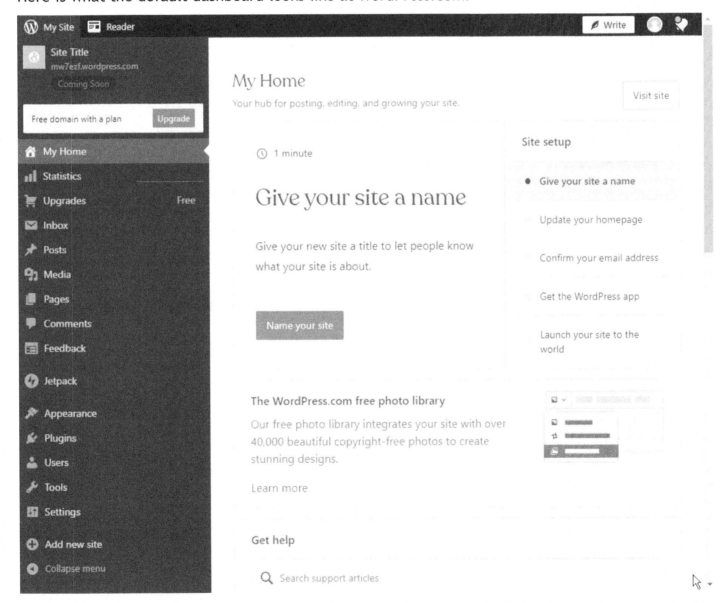

The menu on the left won't be identical to the one in this book. You'll have some items we don't, and we'll have a lot of features you don't. For comparison, here is the default dashboard of a WordPress.org site:

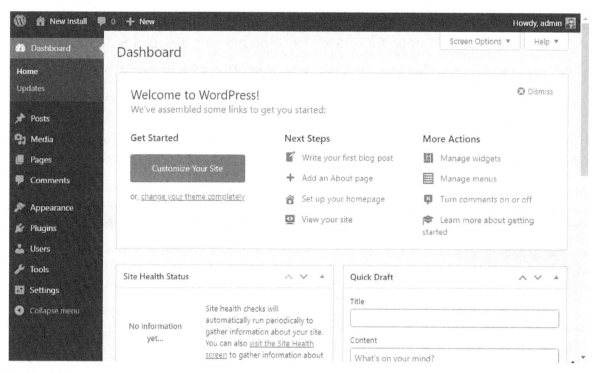

Most of the menu items on the left are present in both versions, but you can clearly see the differences in appearance. Those differences become more pronounced as you open those sub-menus. For example, if you click on the Settings menu in both versions, these are the screens you would see:

WordPress.com Settings page:

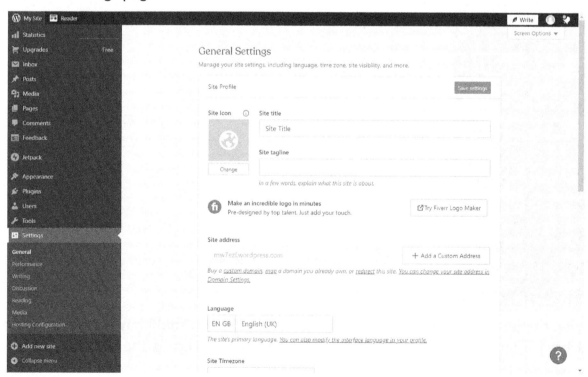

In WordPress.org it looks like this:

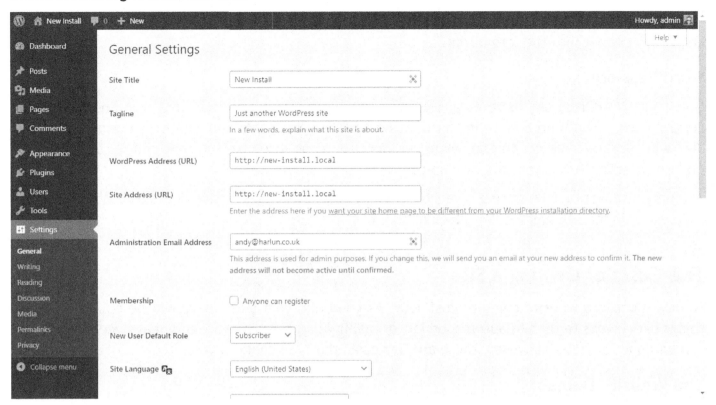

The same kind of information is shown in both settings screens, but the WordPress.com version is more user-friendly, designed with the less-technical users in mind. You'll see this throughout that dashboard. You may like that, but remember I said there are limitations in all but the most expensive subscription plans. You will be restricted in what you can do on the site and what you can install into WordPress. For example, on the free plan, you cannot put adverts, but Wordpress can put their own adverts on your site. You also won't be able to install any theme or plugin you want. You can check out the complete list of features on each of the paid plans on their pricing page:

https://wordpress.com/pricing/

ON that page, you'll see that it's only when you get up to the eCommerce plan at $45 per month are most of the limitations removed. Remember this if you use WordPress.com as you go through the book, because not everything I describe will be available to you.

By comparison, a WordPress site using the .org version can be setup from around $3 per month without any limitations. My web hosting page shows how to set this all up with a WordPress recommended host, and a discount I've negotiated for you:

https://ezseonews.com/hosting

Think of the difference between WordPress.com and WordPress.org as being similar to renting or owning a house. When you rent a house, there are limits to what you can do to it, and you can be thrown out at any time. When you own the building outright, you can do whatever you want with it, and no one can tell you how to design, decorate, or renovate *your* home.

Let's dive deeper into the .org option.

WordPress.org

Going the WordPress.org route means you can start building a site that YOU own and have total control over.   You'll be able to install whatever plugins you want, and whatever theme you want. You will also be able to choose whatever domain name you like, so you could call your site AndysAGreatTeacher.com if it's available.

The only disadvantage of setting up a site with the WordPress.org version is that it's not free. The costs are minimal, though, so let's look at them.

The Costs of Owning a Site

So how much is a website going to cost you? As you build your site, there will be optional costs - things like a website theme, autoresponder, or mailing list, but these are optional since most things can be done for free. However, there are two costs that you cannot avoid.

The Website Domain

The website domain is your site's address on the internet. **Google.com** is the website domain of our favorite search engine. **CNN.com** is the domain of a popular international news service.

You will need to buy a domain for your website. We'll look at this later, but for now, let's just consider the price. Typically, a domain name will cost around $10 per year. You can sometimes get the first year for free when you buy web hosting, but once that first year is up, you'll be paying $10 per year to keep your domain name alive.

Your domain name will be registered with a company called a registrar. It is the registrar that will collect the $10 payment every year. The registrar can be the same company that you use for your web hosting or a different company. We'll look at the pros and cons of both options later.

Website Hosting

Your website needs to be "hosted" on a special type of computer called a server. Servers are connected to the internet 24/7. We call the companies that lease or rent space out on these servers "web hosts." A web host's job is to make sure their servers are up, running, and well always maintained.

Since you want to create a website, you need to rent some disk space from a web host on one of these servers. This is a monthly fee from as little as $3.00 per month (although it does vary greatly between web hosts).

As mentioned earlier, some web hosts offer a free domain name (for the first year). They can offer a free domain name because you pay them a monthly fee for web hosting; therefore, they get their investment back over time. To take advantage of the free domain offers, you will need to use that web host as the registrar of your domain, which I don't recommend (see later).

So, the total essential costs of running your website are:

1. $10 per year for the domain name.
2. $3 per month for web hosting.

That's a total of under $50 per year.

Note, these prices are those that were available from my hosting page (mentioned above) at the time of writing.

Registrar & Web Hosts

When you sign up with a web host, they will offer to be your domain registrar as well. The advantage is that all the bills you receive are from the same company, meaning you only have to deal with ONE company.

There are disadvantages to this arrangement, though, and many people (including myself) prefer to keep host and registrar separate.

Potential problem: If for any reason your web host decides your website is causing them problems (i.e., they get spam complaints, or your website is using up too many system resources), they can take your site down without any warning. What happens next?

If you use a combined web host and registrar, it goes something like this:

1. Your site goes down.
2. You contact your host, and they tell you that they received spam complaints about your domain.
3. They refuse to put your site back up.
4. You need to move your site to a new host, but your existing web host is the registrar and can make that difficult.
5. Your site remains down for a long time while you sort things out and eventually move the site to a new host and registrar.

Time to resolve this? Weeks or months.

OK, let's see what happens if your registrar is separate from your host.

1. Your site goes down.
2. You contact your host, and they tell you that they received spam complaints from your

domain.

3. They refuse to put your site back up.

4. You order hosting with a different company and copy your site to the new host.

5. You log in to your registrar account and change the name servers to the new host. This takes seconds to do.

Time to resolve this? Your site is back up within hours on the new web host.

This is one scenario where using a separate host and registrar is important.

Another scenario, which doesn't bear thinking about, is if your hosting company goes out of business (it does happen sometimes). What becomes of your site? Well, you probably lose it AND your domain name if your hosting company is also your registrar.

If your registrar and host are two separate companies, you'd simply get hosting somewhere else and change the name servers at your registrar. With this arrangement, your site would only be down for 24 hours or less. You might be asking what happens if the registrar goes out of business? Well that's where choosing an established company comes in. I have used the same registrar for over a decade, and it's the one I recommend on my hosting page. They control all of my domains.

Another situation that I have heard about is when a hosting company locks you out of your control panel (a login area where you can administer your domain(s)) because of a dispute over something. That means you cannot possibly move the domain to a new host because you must have access to that control panel to do it. Consequently, your domain will be down for as long as the dispute takes to resolve.

A final word of caution! I have heard horror stories of people not being able to transfer their domain out from a bad web host. Even worse than that, the domain they registered at the hosting company was not registered in their name but the name of the hosting company.

For all the above reasons, when you are ready to buy hosting, please consider using a separate web host and registrar. I'll show you exactly how to set this up, so you do not have to figure this out on your own.

However, if you just want the easy option of using one company, I'll show you how to do that as well.

The Domain Name

When you decide to put a website online, you will need a domain name. The domain name is the "address" that identifies your site. For example, the domain name of my main site is ezseonews.com. If you type that into a web browser, you will be taken to my site.

In this chapter, I want you to decide on your domain name. That means choosing one and making sure it is available.

The process goes a little like this:

1. Decide on the topic of your site.

2. Brainstorm some ideas for a domain name.

3. Check if your ideas are available.

4. Buy the domain.

The last part (buying the domain) can wait until the next chapter but don't wait too long after finding the one you want. Good domains don't remain available for long.

Once you know what your site will be about, the best way to brainstorm ideas is to sit down with a paper and pen and start scribbling. Write down anything that comes to mind.

For example, if your site offered advice to homeowners on how to make their home more eco-friendly, your scribbling might include words like:

Green, eco-friendly, off-grid, home improvements, energy, solar, heating, materials, recycling, efficient, environment, carbon footprint

From that list, you'd then try to come up with some ideas for domain names. Let's say:

ReduceYourCarbonFootprint.com
GreenHomeImprovements.com
EcoHomeEfficiency.com
EfficientGreenHome.com

Once you have a lot of ideas, it is time to check if any of them are available.

I use a free tool called Domain Name Analyzer (https://domainpunch.com/dna/), which allows me to type in as many ideas as I want and see if they are available. If you search Google for it, you should find it for PC or Mac.

I entered my domains from above and asked the software to check .com, .net, and.co.uk versions of the site. Here are the results:

#	Domain	Status	IP	Whois Lookup At	TLD
✅ 1	EfficientGreenHome.co.uk	Available		14/12/2020 14:31:19	uk
✅ 2	EfficientGreenHome.net	Available		14/12/2020 14:31:07	net
✅ 3	EfficientGreenHome.com	Available		14/12/2020 14:31:07	com
✅ 4	EcoHomeEfficiency.co.uk	Available		14/12/2020 14:31:07	uk
✅ 5	EcoHomeEfficiency.net	Available		14/12/2020 14:31:19	net
✅ 6	EcoHomeEfficiency.com	Available		14/12/2020 14:31:07	com
7	GreenHomeImprovements.co.uk	NA [Resolves]	23.236.62.147	14/12/2020 14:31:04	uk
✅ 8	GreenHomeImprovements.net	Available		14/12/2020 14:31:07	net
9	GreenHomeImprovements.com	NA [Resolves]	185.224.137.125	14/12/2020 14:31:07	com
10	ReduceYourCarbonFootprint.co.uk	NA [Resolves]	217.160.0.130	14/12/2020 14:31:10	uk
✅ 11	ReduceYourCarbonFootprint.net	Available		14/12/2020 14:31:19	net
12	ReduceYourCarbonFootprint.com	NA [Resolves]	217.160.0.130	14/12/2020 14:31:10	com

I got lucky here. Several of my ideas were available.

A word of advice. Don't get discouraged when you find most, if not all, of your ideas have already been taken. Just carry on brainstorming, and you will find that perfect domain name.

The domain TLD

The part of the domain at the end is called the TLD (Top Level Domain).

There are hundreds of different types of TLD these days, but my advice (and it is only advice, so ignore it if you want to) on choosing one is to avoid the gimmicky TLDs like .cheap, .expert, .free,. monster, .now, etc., and choose one of the main TLDs.

Here is my process for deciding on the TLD:

1. If your site is the site of an organization, use .org, otherwise

2. If your site is for a worldwide audience, use .com, otherwise

3. If your site is for your own country only, use the TLD for your country, e.g., .co.uk in the UK, .de for Germany, etc.

Once you have found your desired domain name, proceed to the next chapter, where I'll give you instructions on buying the domain and hosting, and set up WordPress.

Tasks to Complete

1. Find a domain name that you like and is available.

Domain, Host, Registrar & Installing WordPress

There are many web hosts out there, and many have their own methods for installing WordPress. To make things worse, the installation and setup process can change, often without notice.

As I write this book, I am acutely aware of what happens when things change. Suddenly, I get a lot of emails from readers asking for help because the book is wrong. This happened in the 2020 version of the book. I created a comprehensive tutorial showing how to install WordPress on a web host, only for things to change weeks after the book was published. Thankfully I have the updates page (covered earlier), which all readers can access, so I could address those issues. However, I still got a lot of emails from readers who had forgotten about that page.

So, from the 2021 version of this book, I started to do things differently based on two facts:

1. The world of hosts and registrars can change quickly, meaning that information can quickly become out of date.

2. The installation process is very visual. I've had a lot of feedback from readers (and students on my courses), asking for video tutorial instead of written instructions.

I decided to create a page on my site where you can access up-to-date tutorials on getting hosting, a registrar, and installing WordPress. If something changes during the year, I can update those tutorials. Therefore, you will always have up to date information.

You can access this page here:

https://ezseonews.com/whr

This page has links to 3 different tutorials. You only need to follow one of these tutorials based on your requirements.

1. You want to use a separate host and registrar (recommended).

2. You want to use the same company as host and registrar.

3. You already have hosting and just need to install WordPress.

When you are ready to get started, go to this page and decide which option you want to follow.

Tasks to Complete

1. Follow the relevant tutorials to get the domain and hosting set up, and install WordPress.

Log In and Out of Your Dashboard

Go and look at your website in a web browser by typing the domain URL into the address bar or simply clicking the link provided on completion of the installation.

You should see your WordPress site up and running. Of course, it won't have any of your content yet, and it does come pre-installed with a few web pages you'll need to delete, but you should see the homepage displaying a "Hello World!" post.

Before we start learning how to configure the site, let's just log in and then log out again, so we know how.

You should have already bookmarked the login URL, but if not, just add **/wp-admin** (or **wp-login.php**) to the end of the URL, e.g.

https://mydomain.com/wp-admin

You'll be taken to the login screen:

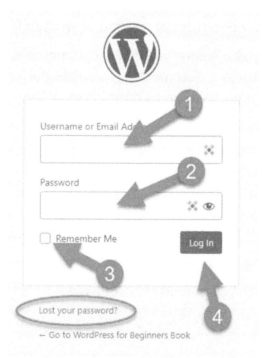

Enter the **username** and **password** you chose when installing WordPress, check the **Remember Me** checkbox, and then click the **Log In** button.

The "Remember Me" box ensures that your username and password will be automatically entered next time you log in to your Dashboard from your computer.

NOTE: If you ever forget your password, you can click the link under the login boxes to reset your password. The reset instructions will be sent to your admin email address (that's the one you entered when installing WordPress).

After logging in, you'll find yourself inside the Dashboard. You can have a look around, but don't go changing anything just yet. Don't worry if it looks a little daunting in there. We'll take a tour of the Dashboard, and I'll show you step-by-step, with screenshots, how to set it all up so you can have a great looking website.

For now, let's log out, so you are clear on how to do that.

Move your mouse over the top right where it says "Howdy, Your name." Note that Howdy is an American word for "Hi," so you may see a different greeting there.

A menu will appear:

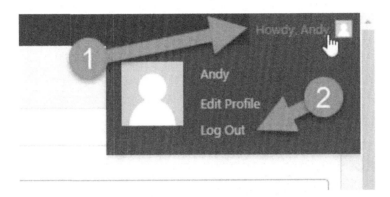

Click the "Log Out" link.

You'll be logged out and taken back to the login screen.

Great, WordPress is installed, and you know how to log in and out of the Dashboard.

Tasks to Complete

1. Install WordPress.
2. Log in, have a quick look around the Dashboard, then log out.

WordPress Web Pages

Before we start delving into WordPress's inner workings and build our site, I need to talk for a moment about web pages because WordPress does things in a way that confuses a lot of people. And it is not just beginners that can get confused. Professional web designers that move to WordPress from other platforms can also struggle with this. So, let's start at the beginning.

Websites are made up of web pages. You can think of a web page as a single page of content.

When you want to add a piece of content to your website, e.g., an article, contact form, etc., you need to create a web page to put it on. In WordPress, there are two ways we can create a web page. We can use a WordPress **POST** or a WordPress **PAGE**.

I'll go into the differences between these two types of web pages later. For now, just realize that these two options exist.

To complicate matters further, WordPress will create some web pages all by itself to help organize your content.

With a WordPress website, you'll have a homepage, some web pages you create, and some web pages that WordPress creates.

Here is a simplified diagram to help explain the organization of a WordPress website:

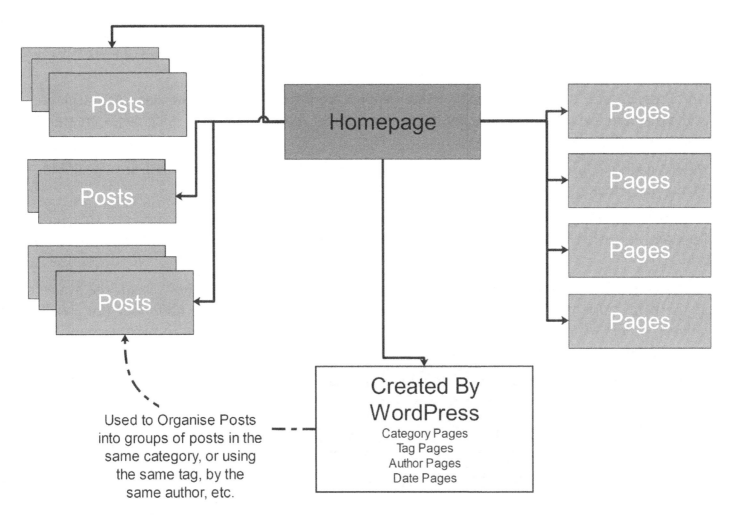

The homepage is a very special page on any website. It can often rank highly in the search engines and can be used to introduce your site to new visitors, guiding them around the website.

We've then got the two types of web pages that you create. We've got pages created as WordPress **posts**, and pages created as WordPress **pages**. The way I have drawn them, hints at their use.

Let's start off with pages. These are pretty much standalone pieces of content that are largely unrelated to any other piece of content on the site. A typical use for pages includes "Privacy Policy," "Terms," "Contact Us," and "About Us" pages. You can also use a WordPress page as your homepage, and this is the one exception to a page being largely unrelated to the other content on the site.

Posts are a completely different beast altogether. If you think about a typical website, you'll often see content organized into "groups" or "categories" on the site. For example, a site on amateur radio may have several articles, each reviewing a different Kenwood Radio. These web pages would likely be grouped into a category called "Kenwood". There might be another bunch of articles, each reviewing a different Yaesu radio. These articles are logically grouped into a category called "Yaesu". WordPress would automatically create a category page for Kenwood that lists all posts in that category, and another for Yaesu. If someone comes to the site looking for Yaesu radio reviews, they can visit the Yaesu category page. It will list all Yaesu reviews on the site, typically with the title, a short description, and a link to view the entire review.

WordPress "posts" are used for content that benefits from grouping and organizing. As you can see in the diagram above, "posts" are organized in a number of different ways using pages created by WordPress (often called archive pages).

We will go into a lot more detail on categories later in the book. We will also look at tags, but let's have a quick look at them now.

From the diagram, you can see that WordPress will create tag pages to help organize your posts. Tags are essentially another organizational tool that you have and they complement categories brilliantly.

You can think of tags as very important "keywords" that are related to your post. Using the example of the ham radios again, I might tag some review articles with the tag **handheld** (i.e., walkie talkies), others with **mobile** (i.e., to be installed in a car), and yet others with **base** (to be used as base stations).

WordPress will create a "tag page" for every tag you create and provide links to all the posts that use that tag.

The **Handheld** tag page will list all articles where the **handheld** tag has been used, so it will basically list all walkie talkie style radio. That might include radios from different categories.

Tags are a secondary method of organizing posts.

Why this level of categorization is important will become obvious when we look at these topics in more detail later.

As you create posts, WordPress will also create author and date archives. An author archive is a page that lists all posts by an author. Can you guess what a date archive is? Yup. It's a page that lists all posts made on a particular date.

As you can see, WordPress is working in the background, creating multiple pages to help organize the content on your website. That's one of the reasons why WordPress is called a Content Management System, or CMS.

Pre-Installed WordPress Themes

Before we continue, I need to mention something very important.

WordPress uses something called a theme to control the layout, color, fonts, and general design of your site. To get you started, WordPress pre-installs a few themes and sets one of them as default. The theme is not WordPress. The theme is simply an add-on to WordPress. It doesn't affect the core functionality of WordPress or the content you create. It just defines how your content is displayed to your visitor, so we're talking colors, fonts, etc. You can change the theme at any time (in seconds) and won't lose any of the content you have created. The new theme will just have its own ideas on how to display your content. You can think of themes as website skins.

You can only have one theme active on your site at any one time.

WordPress creates a new theme every year and names it after the year. In late 2021 or early 2022, we are expecting the release of the Twenty Twenty-Two theme. However, it's likely that this theme will only be compatible with WordPress 5.9 or later, and some of my readers will be on earlier versions of WordPress. With that in mind, I've decided to stick with the Twenty Twenty-One theme for this version of the book, so you don't have cross-version compatibility problems.

If you decide to use a different theme as you go through the book, you may see design options that I don't have and vice versa. That is OK. You might just need to refer to the documentation that comes with your theme to get the most out of it. But understand that whatever theme you use, you'll still be able to follow 100% of this book, so don't start fretting about this.

Since you bought the book to learn WordPress, my advice is to learn WordPress using the Twenty Twenty-One theme so that the screenshots in this book match exactly what you see in your WordPress Dashboard. You can always change the theme later when you start to build a real site.

Delete Un-Used Themes

Go to the **Appearance** menu on the left and click **Themes** to access the themes management screen. If your instance of WordPress is a new install, you'll probably see 2 or 3 pre-installed themes.

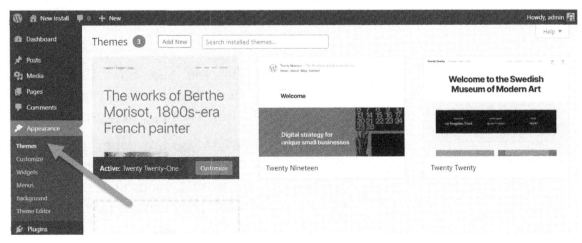

You can see that Twenty Twenty-One is marked as active in my screenshot.

There is also a Twenty Nineteen and a Twenty Twenty theme.

It is a good idea to delete any themes you are not using for security reasons. Old themes may have security holes that hackers can take advantage of. At the very least, keep all installed themes (yes, even the inactive ones) up to date.

Before we delete the unused themes, you might like to have a look and see what they look like.

Move your mouse over the Twenty Nineteen theme, and click the Live Preview button:

The **Customize** screen opens, showing a preview of what that theme will look like if it was the active theme:

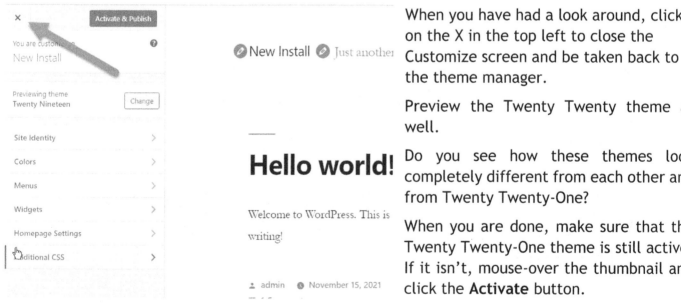

When you have had a look around, click on the X in the top left to close the Customize screen and be taken back to the theme manager.

Preview the Twenty Twenty theme as well.

Do you see how these themes look completely different from each other and from Twenty Twenty-One?

When you are done, make sure that the Twenty Twenty-One theme is still active. If it isn't, mouse-over the thumbnail and click the **Activate** button.

We can now delete the unused themes.

Move your mouse over the Twenty Nineteen theme thumbnail and click the **Theme Details** button.

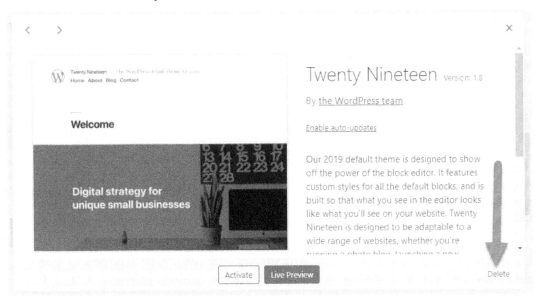

Click the **Delete** link on the details page. You will be asked for confirmation to delete it.

Repeat the process for the other un-used themes, so you are just left with Twenty Twenty-One.

Whoops, I've Deleted the Wrong Theme

Maybe you've decided that you want to use the Twenty Nineteen theme after all, but it's gone. The good news is that you can easily re-install themes from within your Dashboard.

Go to the theme manager screen and click the **Add New** button at the top to be taken to the Add Themes screen:

On the **Add Themes** screen, type the name of the theme you want to re-install:

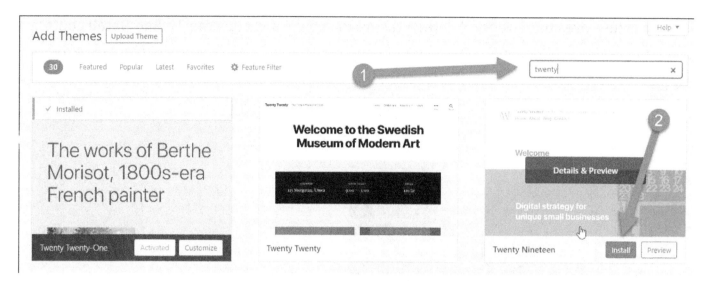

I've just typed **Twenty** in the box, and that was enough to find both themes I deleted, so all I need to do is click the **Install** button and then **Activate** if I want to use that one instead:

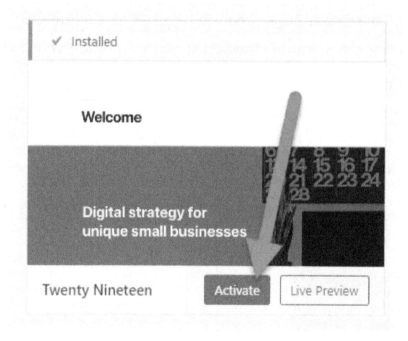

That was easy enough to find, wasn't it?

While on the **Add Themes** screen, explore! Click on the **Latest** link at the top to see the newest themes you can install and use for free.

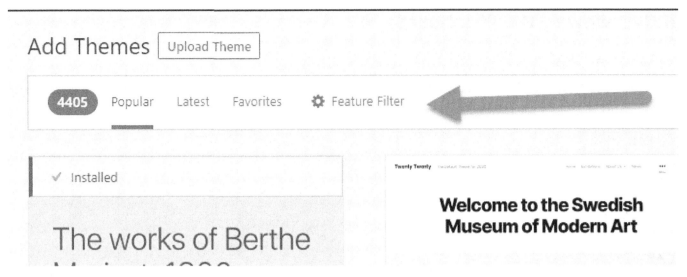

What about that **Feature Filter** page?

Explore the range of free themes on these pages. Install them if you want, but when you are done, remove them all except the one you are using.

In the next chapter, we are going to have a look around the WordPress Dashboard.

An Overview of the Dashboard

When you log in to WordPress, you are presented with the Dashboard. This is what it looks like:

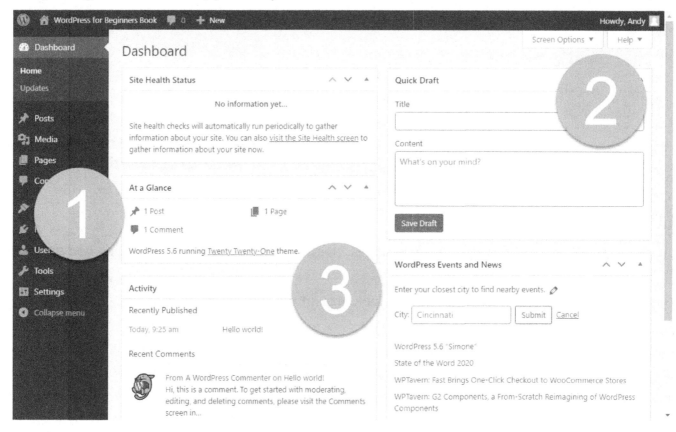

1. The Sidebar
2. Screen Options, Help, Profile & Logout
3. The Main screen

Let's look at each of these in turn.

The Sidebar

The sidebar's purpose is to give you access to the Dashboard navigation menu. This contains all of the tools you need to build, manage, and maintain your website. You can add/edit content on your site, upload images, moderate comments, change your site theme, add/remove plugins, and everything else you will need to do as a website owner. We'll look at these features in detail later in the book.

Screen Options, Help, Profile & Logout

Screen Options is a drop-down menu that allows you to decide what is shown on the various screens within the Dashboard. If you click the Screen Options link, you'll see something like this:

Dashboard

What you see will depend on where you are in the dashboard, the version of WordPress you have installed, installed plugins, and themes. These options are context-sensitive and will be relevant to the current page you are viewing. For example, if you are in the section for moderating comments, the screen options will be relevant to commenting.

By changing these options, you can customize what is displayed on your Dashboard. If you don't want to see something, you simply uncheck it. Be aware that not all areas of the dashboard have screen options.

TIP: When following along with this book, if you find something missing from the screen that should be there, go in and check the screen options to ensure that it's enabled.

We will be popping into the screen options a few times in this book.

To the right of the **Screen Options** is a button to access WordPress help. Clicking it opens a help panel:

The left side of this help panel is tabbed, offering you categorized help sections. Like the screen options, the help panel is context-sensitive, so it shows you the most useful help items for the Dashboard area you are currently working in (I was in the comments section of my Dashboard when

I took this screenshot).

If you need more detailed help, there are links on the right side that take you to the official WordPress documentation and support forums.

Finally, in this area of the Dashboard screen, if you place your mouse over the "Howdy, Your name" top right, a panel opens:

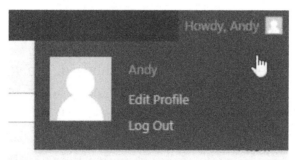

We saw this earlier in the book.

This menu gives you a direct link to edit your profile (which we will fill out later) and a link to log out of your WordPress Dashboard. Whenever you finish a session in the WordPress Dashboard, it's always a good idea to log out.

The Main Screen

This is where all the work takes place. What you see in the main screen area will depend on where you are in the Dashboard. For example, if you are in the comments section, the main screen area will list all the comments people have made on your site. If you are in the themes section, the main screen will display installed themes, and so on. Some of these screens can be customized using screen options (if available) to show/hide elements.

Tasks to Complete

1. Go in and explore the Dashboard to familiarize yourself with the system.

2. Go and check out the pre-installed WordPress Themes.

3. Delete all inactive themes for security reasons.

4. Click on a few of the menu items in the left navigation column and see if screen options are available. If they are, open them and enable/disable some of the checkboxes to see how they relate to what you see in your dashboard. See how the options are related to the page you are viewing in the Dashboard?

5. Have a look at the help options. You won't need any of that now, but it is a good idea to be familiar with these options just in case you get stuck in the future.

Cleaning Out the Pre-Installed Stuff

When you install WordPress, it installs a few default items like the themes we looked at earlier and the "Hello World" post you saw on the homepage. In most cases, you'll also find a "Sample page," a comment, some widgets, and a few plugins. Of course, different web hosts may install, or not, whatever they want. If you don't see everything I show you, or yours is a little different, don't worry. That is normal.

In this chapter, we'll look at the pre-installed content and then delete it. By the end of this chapter, you'll have a fresh, clean, empty website ready for your content.

Deleting the "Hello World" Post

If you visit your site homepage, you'll see that the "Hello World" post is displayed front and center.

To delete the post, we need to use the "Posts" menu from the sidebar navigation.

You can either move your mouse over the word **Posts** and select **All Posts** from the popup menu, like this:

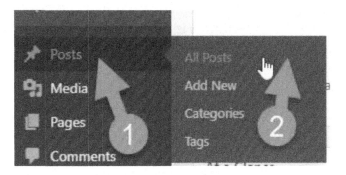

Or you can click the word **Posts,** and the sub-menu will become integrated into the left sidebar. At the same time, WordPress will automatically select the first item in the menu – **All Posts**:

This will open a table of all posts on your site:

This table shows you a list of all posts on your site. Move your mouse over the Hello World! Title. A menu appears allowing you do carry out various actions on the post.

Something to try

Open the **Screen Options** top right and uncheck/check some of the boxes to see how it affects what you see on your screen. Try out the **Extended View** in the **View Mode** section of the screen options (hint: You will need to click the **Apply** button for that to take effect).

Did you see what happened?

One of the things you'll now see is that menu, permanently fixed under the title.

Please leave the screen options in **Extended view** for now. You can change that back later if you want but having that menu visible is a help for what we want to do next.

The extended view used to be called the Excerpt View because it displays an excerpt under the title of the post. More on excerpts later.

Before We Delete It

Let's have a look at it.

Click on the title of the **Hello World** post to open the post editor (also known as Gutenberg).

Note, you may get a popup welcome to the block editor (Gutenberg) so feel free to read that before continuing.

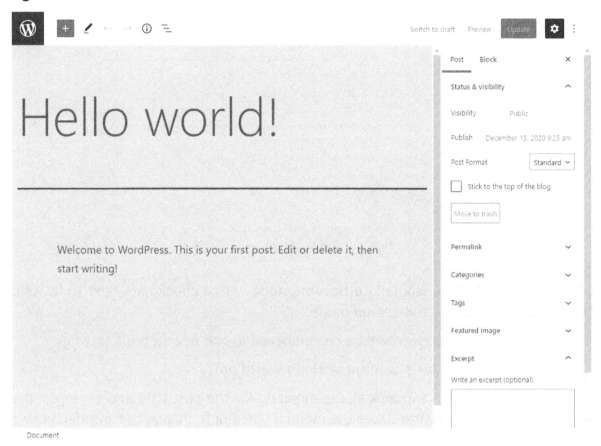

This is where you can edit the post if you want. We won't be doing that now, but I wanted to show you something. WordPress has removed the left sidebar navigation. If this happens to you, don't panic. You can easily get it back by clicking on the WordPress logo in the top left corner:

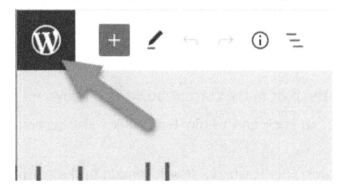

That will take you back to the **All Posts** screen. However, there is a better option.

Click on the **Hello World** post title again to re-open Gutenberg.

In the top right of the Gutenberg editor is a menu button with three vertically arranged dots. Click it:

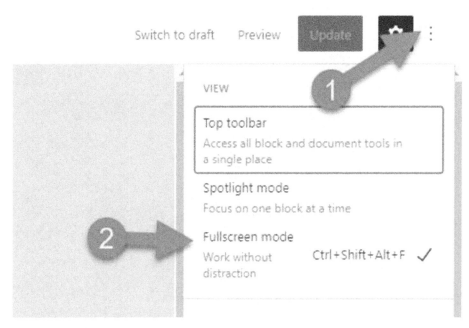

You'll see an item in that menu labeled **Fullscreen mode** with a checkmark next to it. Click on that row in the menu to disable full-screen mode.

The left sidebar menu will re-appear and be remembered as the new default settings.

OK, now you've had some fun, let's delete the Hello World post.

Go back to the **All Posts** screen and look at the menu under the post title and excerpt. (Note that you will need to mouse over the title to see the menu if you didn't change to extended view earlier).

This menu allows you to:

1. **Edit** the post – Go to the full edit screen with the post loaded for editing.

2. **Quick Edit** - allows you to edit some details of the post, but not all. Click it to see the quick edit panel. You can click the **Update** or **Cancel** button to close it when you are done.

3. **Trash** (or bin, or whatever that word is in the language your WordPress is using) – lets you delete it.

4. **View** – which will open the post in the current browser window.

We want to delete the post, so click on the bin/trash link. The screen will refresh, and the post will be gone.

If you accidentally delete a post, don't worry. It will remain in the trash until you empty the trash. I actually want to keep the "Hello World!" post on my site so that I can use it later in the book, so let's undelete the post.

To do this, look for the **Trash** link above the table of posts.

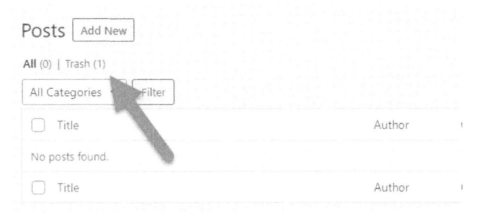

There is a (1) next to it. That means there is one item in the trash (my "Hello World" post). If you click on the **Trash(1)** link, you'll be taken to the trash, where you can see all the posts that were sent there.

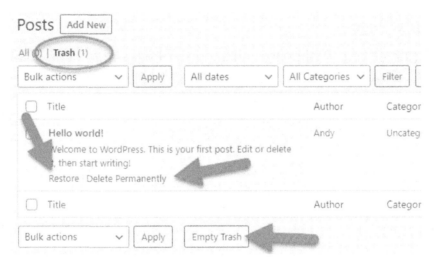

Notice the Trash (1) link is bold to indicate you are on that "tab."

The menu under the title and excerpt gives you two options. **Restore** the post (i.e., undelete it), or **Delete Permanently**.

If you have a lot of posts in the trash and you want to delete them all, click the **Empty Trash** button underneath he table.

NOTE: When WordPress created the "Hello World!" post, it also added a demo comment to the post. When you deleted the post, the comment was also deleted because it belonged to that post. When you undelete (restore) a post, any comments that were deleted with the post are also restored.

I am going to click on the **Restore** link to undelete the Hello World post and comment. You can do the same if you wish. You know how to delete it when you decide you want to.

Now, if I go to the **Comments** page (menu on the left of the dashboard), you can see that comment in the table:

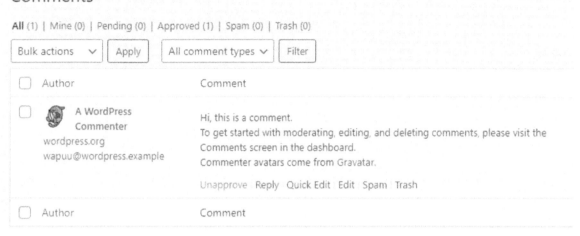

Deleting the Sample Page

In the sidebar navigation of your Dashboard, click on the **Pages** menu link. This will open the first item in that menu - **All Pages**.

Like the posts section, this will bring up a list of all pages on the site. There will probably be two:

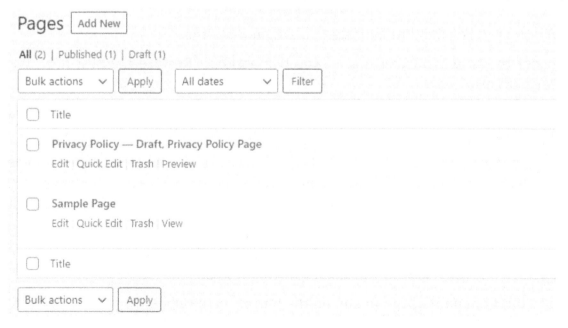

You'll notice that across the top of the table, we are told the status of the pages. There are two pages in total, as shown by the **All(2)**. One is published - **Published (1),** and one is a draft - **Draft (1)**. These status indicator links are filters. Clicking on the **Published (1)** link will filter only those pages that are published and display them in the table. Clicking on **Draft (1)** will show only those draft pages.

You have already seen similar status indicators though I didn't mention them at the time. Can you remember where?

That's right. On the **All Posts** screen and **Comments** screen. Go to these areas of the dashboard and check them out for yourself. They can be useful for quickly managing your content.

OK, back to the **All Pages** screen.

You'll notice that in the list of pages, the **Privacy Policy** page is labeled as **Draft** because it hasn't been published yet. It is a work in progress. Don't delete this one, as we will make use of that later.

Click the **Trash** link under the **Sample Page.**

As with posts, pages remain in the trash until it's emptied, so they too can be restored if required.

Deleting Widgets

WordPress probably installed several widgets into your dashboard. A widget is simply a "feature" that you can add to your website in predefined areas of the page, e.g., the sidebar, footer, etc.

You may see them if you look at your website:

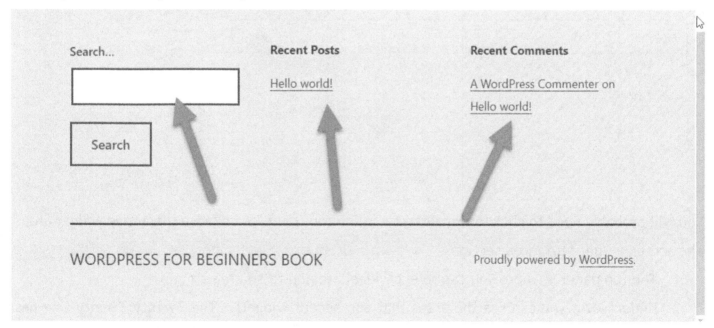

There are three widgets pre-installed in my dashboard:

- The first widget adds a search box.

- The second adds a list of recent posts.

- The third shows the recent comments on the site.

You may not see them all if you deleted the Hello World post. I restored mine, which is why you see both the **Recent Posts** and **Recent Comments** widgets.

Let's explore the widgetized areas, then delete those widgets.

In your Dashboard, move your mouse over the **Appearance** menu, and click on **Widgets**:

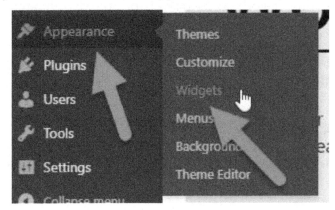

This will take you to the widget screen:

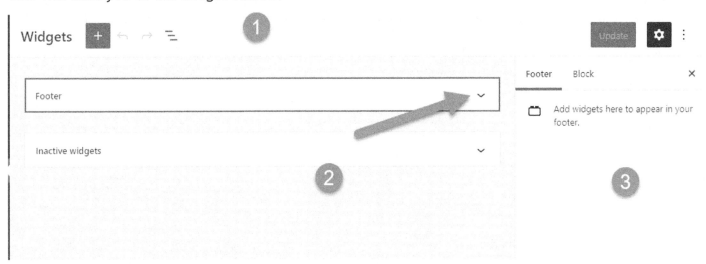

You will probably need to click the small arrow in the top, right, to collapse the active widget area.

The screen is split into three sections.

1. The top panel is where you can select widgets to add to an area.

2. Underneath, you can see the areas that can accept widgets. The Twenty Twenty-One has only one widget area, and that is the footer.   The Inactive widgets section will show any widgets you've created but not used. If you want to remove a widget from an area but think

you might want to use it again later, those widgets can be dragged to this area for safe keeping.

3. On the right, you have access to the widget properties.

If I expand the **Footer** area, I can see any widgets added to the footer:

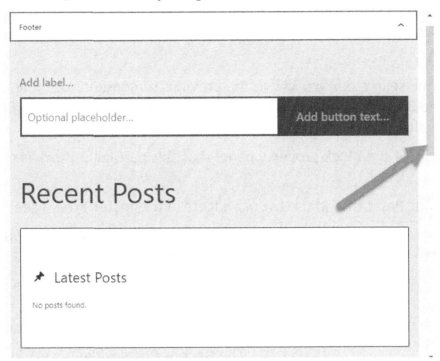

Note the scrollbar on the right because there are several widgets in this area. They correspond to the widgets you see on your site:

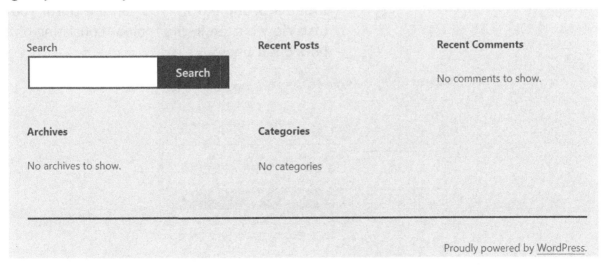

On the **Appearance, Widgets** screen in your Dashboard, clicking on a widget will open its properties in the panel on the right:

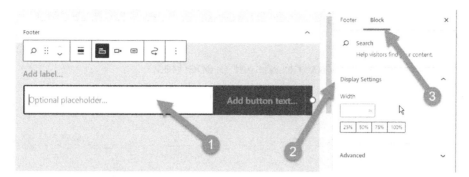

That first widget is the search box you saw in the previous screenshot. You'll notice that these properties are on the **Block** tab of the panel. Widgets are standard Gutenberg Blocks, which as you'll see later, are also the building blocks of the content you will create.

You can see at the top of the **Block** property panel that this particular block is called a **Search** block.

If I click on the **Recent Posts** title in the list of widgets in the footer area, I see:

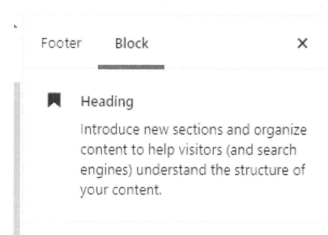

So, the Recent Posts title is added as a **Heading** block.

Click on all the elements you see in the Widgets list and watch the properties panel. You'll see that the widgets are created using different types of blocks.

The **Recent Posts** widget is made up of a **Heading**, and **Latest Posts** Block. To make handling these easier, those two blocks are grouped together, inside a **Group** block. You can see this if you click **List View** button in the toolbar consisting of three horizontal lines:

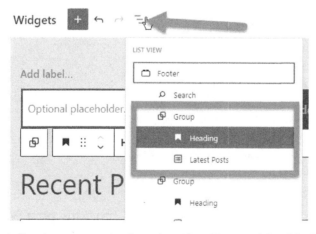

See how **Heading** and **Latest Posts** are nested under the **Group** block? If you click on the **Group** block in that menu, the entire group becomes selected in the widget list:

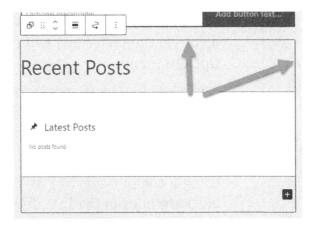

Do you see the box that surrounds the two blocks making up the widget? A menu also appears, and this menu applies to everything in that Group:

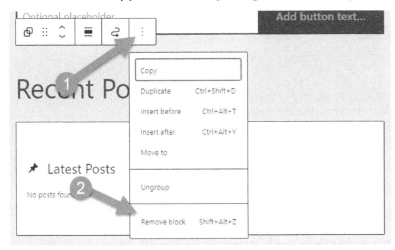

We'll look at the menu in more detail later, but for now, click the **Remove Block** from the **Options** menu on the far right. This will delete the entire group, including the **Heading** and the **Latest Posts** block.

You can also select individual blocks that are part of a group. You can do this from the **List View** menu, or by clicking on the block in the widget list. Either way, you can delete specific blocks inside groups in this way.

Something to try

Click on the **Archives** heading and delete it using the **Options** menu. Repeat for the **Archives** block. What you'll be left with is a **Group** block with nothing inside it:

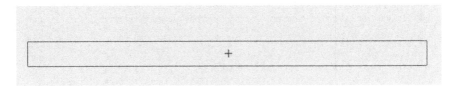

That + inside the group is an invitation to add a block to the group.

You can see this empty Group in the **List View**:

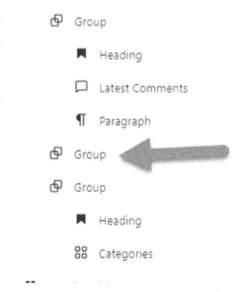

Just like any block, you can select it (directly by clicking it, or via the **List** View) and then delete it using the **Options** menu.

It is possible, though tricky, to select a Group directly within the widget list. You have to click just outside where you think the border of the group would be. Try it. It takes a little practice.

Using a combination of **List View** and direct clicking on blocks/groups in the list, delete them all using the **Options** menu. When you are finished, it'll look something like this:

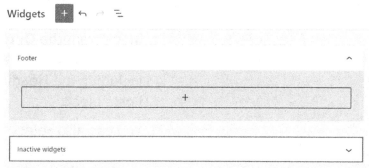

You won't be able to get rid of that last "Group" as it doesn't appear in the **List View**.

Click the **Update** button top right to save your new footer area, then go and visit your site:

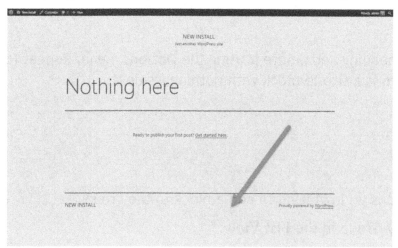

All the widgets are gone!

We'll come back later to look at Widgets in more detail.

A Note About Sidebars

The Gutenberg editor built into WordPress is designed to work with themes that use the full width of the web page to display the content you create in posts and pages. What this means is, most themes created for Gutenberg, like the Twenty Twenty-One theme, don't give you the option of a sidebar.

Many older themes do have the option of a sidebar, and this is one area that was traditionally used for widgets. The problem is Gutenberg doesn't behave properly with these older themes.

Later in this course, I will mention the Classic editor plugin that you can install and use instead of Gutenberg, as it does work well with sidebars. If you decide you want to use a theme with a sidebar, then consider the Classic editor. If, however, you want to embrace changes at WordPress and use Gutenberg, a sidebar free theme is a better choice.

Deleting Plugins

There is one other area we need to check in our dashboard clearout, and that is plugins.

In the sidebar menu, click on **Plugins**. That takes you to the **Installed Plugins** page.

You may or may not have any plugins pre-installed. Two common plugins that are pre-installed on most WordPress installations are the ones shown below:

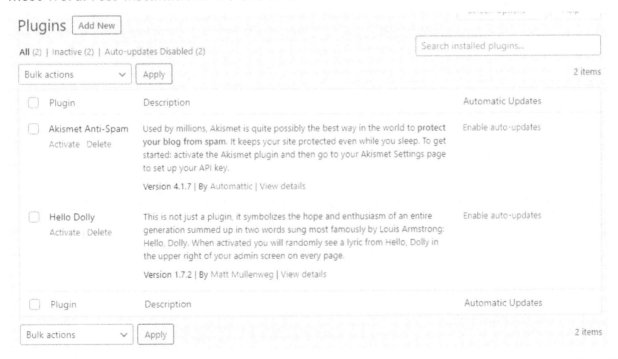

Akismet is a plugin to help you reduce spam. It is a great plugin, but it is only free if your site is not commercial in any way. If you make money from your site, you cannot use it without buying a license. Because of that, I don't cover it in this book.

The other one, Hello Dolly, simply puts quotes from the musical in the toolbar at the top of your dashboard.

You may have other plugins in your installation. Some web hosts will install plugins that are designed to improve speed and reliability on that hosting. If you do have any plugins that include the name of your web host, don't delete them. Everything else can likely be deleted (but ask your host if you are concerned about whether a plugin is essential).

Deleting a plugin properly is a two-step process:

1. If you see a **Deactivate** link under the plugin name, it means the plugin is currently running inside your dashboard.

Hello Dolly
Deactivate

This is not just a plugin, it symbolizes the hope and enthusiasm of a generation summed up in two words sung most famously by Louis ⁊ Hello, Dolly. When activated you will randomly see a lyric from Hello the upper right of your admin screen on every page.

Version 1.7.2 | By Matt Mullenweg | View details

You need to click that deactivate link to turn it off.

2. The **Delete** link will now be visible under the plugin. Click it to delete the plugin. You will be asked to confirm the deletion. Once you confirm, the plugin is removed.

Congratulations, you have cleaned out WordPress and have an empty site waiting for you to move in.

Tasks to Complete

1. Delete the Hello World post and then restore it to see how this works

2. Delete the Hello World post again.

3. Delete the pre-installed Page.

4. Explore the various widgets that WordPress installed and the delete them all.

5. Go to the plugins page and delete all pre-installed plugins, except those that are essential for your hosting (they will include the host's name in the widget title, but ask your host support if you are unsure).

Dashboard Updates

To illustrate points in this chapter, I am going to be using screenshots from an established WordPress site, not the empty site you've seen so far.

WordPress makes it easy for us to know when there are updates. It shows a number in a red circle next to the **Updates** section of the **Dashboard** menu. That number tells you how many updates are available. On this website, there are 7!

Available updates can include plugins, themes, and WordPress itself!

Click on the **Updates** menu item.

At the top of the screen, you'll see a notification whenever there is a new update to WordPress itself. You may also get a warning to update your database and files, so that is always a good precaution to take before an update. Having said that, I rarely do and have never had a problem during an update. Click the link for help on this if you want to do it.

Click on the **Update Now** link to update WordPress if necessary.

Occasionally these WordPress updates will require you to click a button or two, e.g., to update the database. Just follow all screen prompts, and the update will complete and take you back to the Dashboard.

Back on the **Updates** screen, WordPress will be up-to-date, but there may be plugins that need updating. On this site, there are several that need updating:

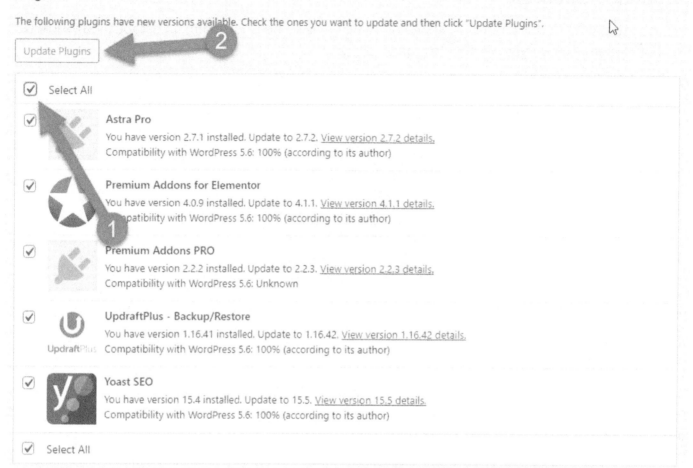

Plugins

The following plugins have new versions available. Check the ones you want to update and then click "Update Plugins".

Update Plugins

☑ Select All

☑ **Astra Pro**
You have version 2.7.1 installed. Update to 2.7.2. View version 2.7.2 details.
Compatibility with WordPress 5.6: 100% (according to its author)

☑ **Premium Addons for Elementor**
You have version 4.0.9 installed. Update to 4.1.1. View version 4.1.1 details.
Compatibility with WordPress 5.6: 100% (according to its author)

☑ **Premium Addons PRO**
You have version 2.2.2 installed. Update to 2.2.3. View version 2.2.3 details.
Compatibility with WordPress 5.6: Unknown

☑ **UpdraftPlus - Backup/Restore**
You have version 1.16.41 installed. Update to 1.16.42. View version 1.16.42 details.
UpdraftPlus Compatibility with WordPress 5.6: 100% (according to its author)

☑ **Yoast SEO**
You have version 15.4 installed. Update to 15.5. View version 15.5 details.
Compatibility with WordPress 5.6: 100% (according to its author)

☑ Select All

You can update all of the plugins by checking the boxes next to each one (the **Select All** checkbox will check them all with a single click) and then click the **Update Plugins** button.

Once the plugin updates have been completed, WordPress will ask you where you want to go next:

Disabling Maintenance mode...

All updates have been completed.

Go to Plugins page | Go to WordPress Updates page

If there are still updates to perform, click the link to return to WordPress updates.

If there are no more updates available, you can click on any of the sidebar menus to go wherever you want.

In my case, there is a theme that needs updating, so back on the updates page, I can update it by checking the box next to it and clicking the **Update Theme** button:

That's all of my updates done.

In the next chapter, we will configure WordPress so that it is ready for our content.

Tasks to Complete

Check to see if there are any updates needing your attention. If there are, go and update everything. Whenever you log in to your Dashboard, if there are updates pending, it is a good idea (for security reasons) to update them immediately.

WordPress Settings

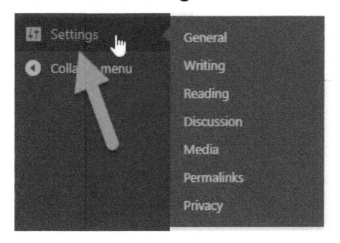

In the sidebar, you'll see an item labeled **Settings**.

Within **Settings,** there are a number of items.

Important: Themes and plugins can add items to the sidebar menu system. If you have items in your menu that are not shown in this book, chances are they have been added by a plugin or theme you installed. The menu system I am going to show you is the core WordPress menu, with no plugins installed and only the Twenty Twenty-One theme.

Let's look at each of these menu items in turn and configure things as we go. By the end of this section, your WordPress settings will be set up with my default settings, which are a great starting point for any site.

General Settings

The General settings page defines some of the basic website settings.

At the top of the screen, the first few settings look like this:

General Settings

Site Title	WordPress for Beginners Book
Tagline	Just another WordPress site
	In a few words, explain what this site is about.
WordPress Address (URL)	http://wordpress-for-beginners-book.local
Site Address (URL)	http://wordpress-for-beginners-book.local
	Enter the address here if you want your site home page to be different from your WordPress installation directory.
Administration Email Address	
	This address is used for admin purposes. If you change this, we will send you an email at your new address to confirm it. The new address will not become active until confirmed.

The information on the General Settings page was filled in when you installed WordPress, and there is probably no reason to change anything.

Right at the top is the **Site Title**. This is usually the same as the domain name but doesn't have to be.

Under the title is the **Tagline**. On some themes, the tagline is displayed in the site header, right under the site name.

You can use the tagline to give your visitors more information about your website. A tagline might be your website's "catchphrase," slogan, mission statement, or just a very brief, one-sentence description.

The next two fields on this settings page are the **WordPress Address (URL)** and the **Site Address (URL),** and you should not change these. The WordPress Address is the URL where WordPress is installed, and the Site Address is the URL you go to view the site in a browser. In most cases, these will be the same value.

Next on this setting page is the **Administration Email Address**. This is very important as you'll get all "admin" notifications sent to this email address. It's also important for something called Gravatars, which we will visit later.

Make sure you use a valid email that you check frequently.

Lower down this General Setting page are these options:

Membership   ☐ Anyone can register

New User Default Role   Subscriber   ∨

The **Membership** option allows visitors to sign up on your site, with their role being defined in the **New User Default Role** drop-down box.

E.g., you could allow visitors to sign up as subscribers or maybe contributors to your site. This can open up a whole can of security worms, so I don't advise you to enable this option. If you want to create a "membership" site, use a dedicated, secure WordPress membership plugin like Wishlist Member (which can turn any WordPress site into a fully-fledged membership site).

The rest of the settings on this page allow you to set the site language, your time zone, date, and time formats.

The timezone is used to timestamp posts on your site correctly. Since we'll look at how you can schedule your posts into the future, the correct time zone will ensure your posts are going out on the intended dates and times.

Select the date and time format you use.

You can also set the day you use for the start of the week. This will be used if you use a calendar widget in your sidebar. If you choose Monday as the start of the week, then Monday will be the first column in the calendar.

If you make any changes to the settings on the General Settings tab, make sure you save the changes when you are finished.

Writing

In the **Settings** menu, click on **Writing**.

The writing settings control the user interface you see when you are adding/editing posts. Let's look at the options.

Here are the first two:

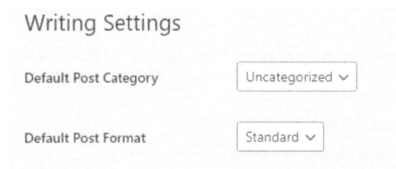

The **Default Post Category** is the category that a post will be assigned to if you don't manually select a category. We haven't set up any categories yet. WordPress set one up for us during installation, called **Uncategorized**, so that is the current default. We'll rename that to something more useful when we look at categories later in the book.

The **Default Post Format** is the default layout/appearance of the posts you add to your site. Different themes will have different post formats you can use. In the Twenty Twenty-One theme, here are your options:

Each of these formats will modify how that post looks, so I recommend you use the Standard option for the default value and then change the format on a post by post basis if needed. I should point out that I rarely change from the default "Standard."

Here are the next few settings:

Post via email

To post to WordPress by email, you must set up a secret email account with POP3 access. Any mail received at this address will be posted, so it's a good idea to keep this address very secret. Here are three random strings you could use: 7wIQ51qG , s8kMXPgn , t6dyAUED .

Mail Server	mail.example.com	Port 110
Login Name	login@example.com	
Password	password	
Default Mail Category	Uncategorized ˅	

The **Post via e-mail** section allows you to set up remote posting. That means you can post content to your site by sending it in as an email. This is beyond the scope of this book.

The final setting on this page is important. It's the update services:

Update Services

When you publish a new post, WordPress automatically notifies the following site update services. For more about this, see Update Services on the Codex. Separate multiple service URLs with line breaks.

    http://rpc.pingomatic.com/

If you see this:

Update Services

WordPress is not notifying any Update Services because of your site's visibility settings.

..then you have checked the **"Search Engine Visibility"** box in the Reading settings. We'll cover that in a moment.

Update services help your content get noticed and included more quickly in the search engines.

WordPress installs just one service, but Pingomatic notifies a lot of other sites, including Google, so that one entry is fine and all I personally use.

You can find larger, ready-made ping lists created by other website owners if you want. Just search Google for "WordPress Ping List," find a list, and paste it into the box.

Don't forget to save if you make changes before moving to the next settings page.

Reading

In the **Settings** menu, click **Reading**.

The reading settings define how your visitors will see certain aspects of your site.

There are only a few settings here, but they are important.

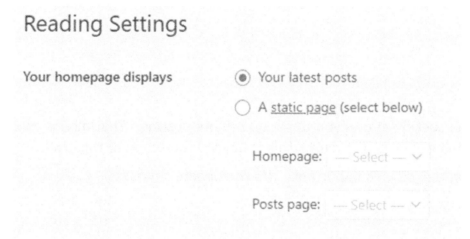

If you have published any WordPress Pages (and WordPress does install a published **Sample** page), you'll see this section at the top. These settings define the content that is seen on your homepage.

The default setting is **Your Latest Posts**. This will display the most recent posts on your homepage. The number of posts displayed on your homepage is determined by whatever you have "Blog pages show at most" set to. Since the default is 10, your last ten posts will appear on your homepage. This type of homepage is common for blogs.

It is possible to set up the homepage like a more traditional website, with a single article forming the basis of the homepage content. You can do this in WordPress by creating a WordPress Page that contains your homepage article. You then select **A Static Page** from the options above and choose the page from the **Homepage** drop-down list. This is typical of business sites, as well as traditional web sites. I'll show you how to do this later.

A little further down we see these:

| Blog pages show at most | 10 | posts |

| Syndication feeds show the most recent | 10 | items |

For each post in a feed, include ◉ Full text
◯ Excerpt

Your theme determines how content is displayed in browsers. Learn more about feeds.

Search engine visibility ☐ Discourage search engines from indexing this site

It is up to search engines to honour this request.

Save Changes

Some pages on your site, like category pages, tag pages, and the homepage, can show lists of posts. These are often called Archive pages. **Blog pages show at most**, defines how many posts appear on those pages.

So, if you have a category on your site called "types of roses," WordPress will create a category page called "Types of Roses." That page will list all posts in that category. If you have 15 articles, each describing a different rose, then WordPress will create two category pages to hold those articles. The first category page will have links to the first 10 (because of the settings above), and the second will list the remaining 5.

I recommend you leave the setting at the default 10.

Syndication feeds show the most recent, refers to your website's RSS feed. Every WordPress site has an RSS feed (in fact, it has many RSS feeds). An RSS feed is just a list of the most recent posts with a link and a description of each post. This setting allows you to define how many of your most recent posts appear in the feed. Again, I recommend 10. We'll look at RSS feeds in more detail later.

For each article in a feed, show, defines what content is shown in the feed. If you select "Full Text," then the complete content of each post is included in the feed. This can make your feed very long and also give spammers a chance to steal your content with tools designed to scrape RSS feeds and post the content to their own sites.

For most websites, I'd recommend you set this to "Summary." That way, only a short summary of each post will be displayed in the feed, which is far less appealing to spammers and easier on the eye for those who genuinely follow your active RSS feeds.

However, if yours is a business site, leaving it as **Full Text** may make more sense since items in the feed will likely be announcements you want to be displayed in their entirety.

Search Engine Visibility allows you to hide your site from the search engines effectively. If you are working on a site that you don't want the search engines to find, you can check this box. Note that if you check this box, you effectively switch off the Update Services section in the writing settings.

I allow search engines to visit and index my site from day 1. Yes, the search engines will find content that is not finished, but that's OK because they'll come back and check the site periodically to pick up changes.

Whether you block the search engines now or not is up to you. Just remember that if you do, your site won't start appearing in the search engines until you unblock them.

I recommend you leave this setting unchecked.

Make sure you click the **Save Changes** button at the bottom if you've edited the settings on the screen.

Discussion

In the **Settings** menu, click **Discussion**.

The discussion settings are related to comments that visitors may leave at the end of your posts. There are a few settings we need to change from the default.

Here are the first few settings in the discussion options:

Discussion Settings

Default post settings	☑ Attempt to notify any blogs linked to from the post
	☑ Allow link notifications from other blogs (pingbacks and trackbacks) on new posts
	☑ Allow people to submit comments on new posts
	(These settings may be overridden for individual posts.)

Attempt to notify any blogs linked to from the article should be left checked. Whenever you write an article and link to another site, WordPress will try to notify that site that you have linked to them. WordPress does this by sending what is called a Ping. Pings will show up in the comment system of the receiving blog and can be approved like a comment. If it is approved, that "pingback" will appear near the comments section on that blog, giving you a link back to your site.

NOTE: Any website can turn pingbacks off. If a ping is sent to a site where pingbacks are OFF, then it won't appear in their comment system.

Here are some example pingbacks published on a web page:

3 Responses to *Men's Health Week Proclamations*

1. **Pingback:** health » Blog Archive » Focus on Men's Health Week This Father's Day : Healthymagination

2. **Pingback:** Focus on Men's Health Week This Father's Day : Healthymagination – health

3. **Pingback:** Focus on Men's Health Week This Father's Day : Healthymagination – men health

Each pingback is a link back to a website that has linked to this webpage.

The next option - **Allow link notifications from other blogs (pingbacks and trackbacks)** allows you to turn pingbacks and trackbacks (trackbacks are very similar to pingbacks) off. If you uncheck this, you will not receive pingbacks or trackbacks.

Should you check it or not?

Well, it's always nice to see when a site is linking to your content. However, there is a technique used by spammers to send fake trackbacks & pingbacks to your site. They are trying to get you to approve their trackback so that your site will then link to theirs.

Personally, I uncheck this option, but if you do leave it checked, I recommend you never approve a trackback or pingback. They are nearly always spam!

Allow people to post comments on new articles should remain checked. It is important that you let your visitors comment on your site's content. A lot of people disable this because they think moderating comments is too much work, but from an SEO point of view, search engines love to see active discussions on websites. Leave it checked!

The next section of options is shown below:

Other comment settings	
	☑ Comment author must fill out name and email
	☐ Users must be registered and logged in to comment
	☐ Automatically close comments on posts older than [14] days
	☑ Show comments cookies opt-in checkbox, allowing comment author cookies to be set
	☑ Enable threaded (nested) comments [5 ∨] levels deep
	☐ Break comments into pages with [50] top level comments per page and the [last ∨] page displayed by default
	Comments should be displayed with the [older ∨] comments at the top of each page

Leave these at their default value (shown above).

The options are self-explanatory but let's go through them quickly.

The first option requires commenters to fill in a name and email. This is very important and often a good indicator of legitimate/spam comments. Spammers tend to fill the name field with keywords (for SEO purposes), whereas legitimate commenters are more likely to use a real name. The email is nice, too, so you can follow up with commenters.

The second item should remain unchecked because we probably do not allow visitors to register and login to our site. We do want *all* visitors to have the option of leaving a comment, though.

The third option allows you to close the comment sections on posts after a certain number of days. I like to leave comments open indefinitely as you never know when someone will find your article and want to have their say. However, if you want to cut back on spam comments, then close comments after a reasonable length of time, say 30 days.

The option to **Show comments cookies opt-in checkbox** is for GDPR compliance and should remain checked if you have any visitors coming from the EU. When checked, a checkbox appears at the bottom of the comment form (on a post), which gives your visitors the option of saving their name, email, and website information in their browser, so it can be used the next time they comment.

Note that you won't see this if you are logged into your dashboard. If you want to see it, visit your hello world post in an incognito browser window.

Threaded (nested) comments should be enabled. This allows people to engage in discussions within the comments section, with replies to previous comments "nested" underneath the comment they are replying to. Here is an example showing how nested comments appear on my site:

You can see that replies to the previous comment are nested underneath, making it clear that the comments are part of a conversation.

The last two options in this section relate to how comments are displayed on the page. If you want, comments can be spread across multiple pages, with, say, 50 comments per page (default). However, I leave this option unchecked so that all comments for an article appear on the same page. If you find that you get hundreds of comments per article (which will slow down the load time of the page), you might want to enable this option, so pages load faster.

The final option in this section allows you to choose whether you want older or newer comments at the top of the comments section.

I prefer comments listed in the order in which they are submitted, as that makes more sense to me. Therefore, I'd leave the setting as "older."

The next section of these settings is shown below:

Email me whenever	☑ Anyone posts a comment
	☐ A comment is held for moderation
Before a comment appears	☑ Comment must be manually approved
	☐ Comment author must have a previously approved comment

You can choose to be notified via email when someone posts a comment and/or when a comment is held for moderation. The way I suggest you set up your site is that all comments are held for moderation, so effectively, those two options are the same thing.

Check one or other of these two options, so you know when there are comments waiting for approval. When you get an email notification, you can then log in to your Dashboard and either approve the comment (so it goes live on your site) or send it to trash if it's blatant spam.

The second two options shown above relate to when a comment can appear on the site. Check the box next to **Comment must be manually approved**. This will mean ALL comments must be approved by you before appearing on the site.

The second option will allow you to auto-approve comments by commenters that have had previous comments approved (i.e., trusted commenters). I recommend you leave this option unchecked for reasons I will explain in a moment. If you did want to use this feature, the first option would need to be unchecked.

So why do I not recommend this option?

A hacking technique (zero-day exploit) targeted sites that were set up to auto-approve comments once a first comment was approved. Hackers would get a harmless comment approved and then post a comment that contained malicious JavaScript. The JavaScript comment would never be manually approved on its own, but with the first comment already approved, it would get automatic approval.

The **Comment Moderation** settings are not important to us since all comments will be moderated. Therefore you can leave these alone.

Comment Moderation

Hold a comment in the queue if it contains [2] or more links. (A common characteristic of comment spam is a large number of hyperlinks.)

When a comment contains any of these words in its content, author name, URL, email, IP address, or browser's user agent string, it will be held in the moderation queue. One word or IP address per line. It will match inside words, so "press" will match "WordPress".

If you do not want to moderate all comments manually, you can use these settings to automatically add a comment to the moderation queue IF it has a certain number of links in it (default is 2), OR the comment contains a word that is listed in the big box.

The **Disallowed Comment Keys** box (previously called comment blacklist) allows you to set up a blacklist to reject comments automatically.

Disallowed Comment Keys

When a comment contains any of these words in its content, author name, URL, email, IP address, or browser's user agent string, it will be put in the Trash. One word or IP address per line. It will match inside words, so "press" will match "WordPress".

Essentially any comment that contains a word or URL listed in this box, or comes from an email address or IP address listed in this box, will automatically be sent to the trash.

That means you can set up your blacklist with "unsavory" words, email addresses, URLs, or IP addresses of known spammers, and you'll never see those comments in your moderation queue. The comment blacklist can significantly cut down on your comment moderation, so I suggest you do a search on Google for **WordPress comment blacklist** and use a list that someone else has already put together (you'll find a few). Just copy and paste their list into the box and save the settings.

The final section of the discussion options is related to Avatars:

Avatars

An avatar is an image that follows you from weblog to weblog appearing beside your name when you comment on avatar enabled sites. Here you can enable the display of avatars for people who comment on your site.

Avatar Display

☑ Show Avatars

Maximum Rating

◉ G — Suitable for all audiences

◯ PG — Possibly offensive, usually for audiences 13 and above

◯ R — Intended for adult audiences above 17

◯ X — Even more mature than above

An Avatar is an image/photo that can appear next to the commenter's name if they have set up something called a Gravatar (which we will revisit later).

I think it is nice to see who is leaving comments, so I recommend you leave Avatars on (**Show Avatars** checked).

For most websites, you should have the maximum rating set to G. This will then hide any Avatars that are not suitable for all visitors. Avatars are assigned ratings when you create them over at Gravatar.com, so this rating system is only as good as the honesty of the person creating the avatar.

The final setting allows you to define the default action if someone does not have an Avatar set up for their email address.

I personally select **Blank** so that no avatar is shown as I think it looks better than one with a load of "mystery person" (or other) generated avatars. However, the choice is yours.

When you have finished with these settings, save the changes.

Media

Click on the **Media** link in the **Settings** menu.

The media settings relate to images and other media that you might insert into your site.

Image sizes

The sizes listed below determine the maximum dimensions in pixels to use when adding an image to the Media Library.

| Thumbnail size | Width | 150 |
| | Height | 150 |

☑ Crop thumbnail to exact dimensions (normally thumbnails are proportional)

| Medium size | Max Width | 300 |
| | Max Height | 300 |

| Large size | Max Width | 1024 |
| | Max Height | 1024 |

These first few settings allow you to define the maximum dimensions for the thumbnail, medium, and large images. You can leave these at their default settings.

The final option asks whether you want your uploaded images to be organized into month- and year-based folders.

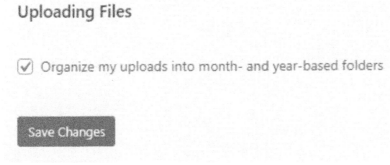

Uploading Files

☑ Organize my uploads into month- and year-based folders

Save Changes

I'd recommend you leave this checked, just so your images are organized into dates on your server. This can help you find the images later if you need to.

Permalinks

Click on the **Permalinks** item in the **Settings** menu.

The Permalink settings define how the URLs (web addresses) are structured for the web pages on your site. We want the URLs on our site to help visitors and search engines.

Permalink Settings

WordPress offers you the ability to create a custom URL structure for your permalinks and archives. Custom URL structures can improve the aesthetics, usability, and forward-compatibility of your links. A number of tags are available, and here are some examples to get you started.

Common Settings

○ Plain   `http://wordpress-for-beginners-book.local/?p=123`

○ Day and name   `http://wordpress-for-beginners-book.local/2020/12/15/sample-post/`

○ Month and name   `http://wordpress-for-beginners-book.local/2020/12/sample-post/`

○ Numeric   `http://wordpress-for-beginners-book.local/archives/123`

◉ Post name   `http://wordpress-for-beginners-book.local/sample-post/`

○ Custom Structure   `http://wordpress-for-beginners-book.local`
                         `/%postname%/`

Available tags:

`%year%` `%monthnum%` `%day%` `%hour%` `%minute%` `%second%`

`%post_id%` `%postname%` `%category%` `%author%`

By default, **Post name** is selected, meaning the URLs of your pages will be the domain name, followed by a forward slash and then the post name, e.g., Acme-inc.com/services

If you are building a site where categories are not a major part of your site structure, I'd recommend you keep this option.

If your site is going to be making good use of categories and posts, I'd recommend your URLs contain the category as well.

Select the **Custom Structure** option at the bottom of the list and click on any pre-selected buttons to turn them off. In this case, click on %postname% to disable it:

Now click on the **%category%** button followed by the **%postname%** button, and your permalink structure will end up as:

`/%category%/%postname%/`

Save the changes.

The URLs on your site will now look like this:

http://mydomain.com/category/postname

The last two options on this settings page are shown below:

Optional

If you like, you may enter custom structures for your category and tag URLs here. For example, using `topics` as your category base would make your category links like `http://wordpress-for-beginners-book.local/topics/uncategorized/`. If you leave these blank the defaults will be used.

Category base _____

Tag base _____

Save Changes

I would leave these two boxes empty.

When WordPress creates a category page or a tag page, the URL will include the word "category" or "tag" to tell you that you are on a special type of web page.

For example:

https://mydomain.com/**category**/roses/

.. might be the URL of a category page listing posts about Roses, and:

https://mydomain.com/**tag**/red

.. might be a tag page listing all posts about red roses on the site (i.e., posts that were tagged with the word "red").

These words in the URL help identify the type of page as a category or tag page. That is useful to search engines and visitors.

If you enter a word into the category base or tag base, the URLs will contain the words you enter here, rather than the default "category" & "tag."

Having keywords in your URL can be helpful, BUT, with Google on the warpath against web spammers, I would not even consider entering a category base or tag base. Leave those boxes empty.

Privacy

Finally, click on the **Privacy** link in the **Settings** menu.

The Privacy settings were introduced to help website owners get ready for GDPR compliance. If you don't know what that is, I recommend you research it a little. It is essentially a privacy law. One of the first steps in becoming compliant is to have a good privacy policy that visitors can read. This will tell them what information, if any, your site collects and stores.

The Privacy options allow you to select an existing privacy policy if you already have one or create a new one. When we cleared out the pre-installed pages, we didn't delete the draft privacy policy created by WordPress because I wanted to use it here.

This draft privacy policy, as I mentioned earlier, is a work in progress. If you go and look at it (click on it in the All Pages list), you will see that WordPress includes essential information relating to WordPress itself, but you will need to go through the policy and flesh it out. If you go to **All Pages** and then click on the **Privacy Policy** title, you'll open it in Gutenberg. At the top of that page, WordPress does offer some assistance:

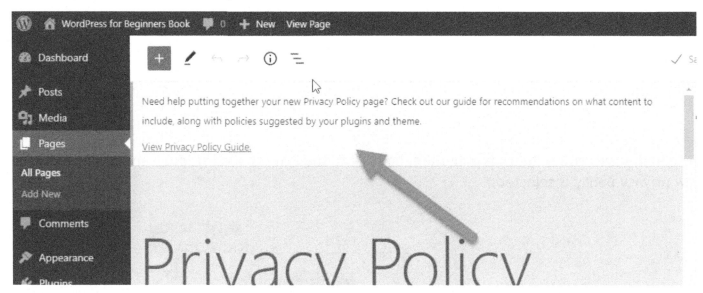

Click that link to **View Privacy Policy Guide** for helpful information on what you should include.

Once your privacy policy is complete, publish the page by clicking the **Publish** button in the top right of the screen:

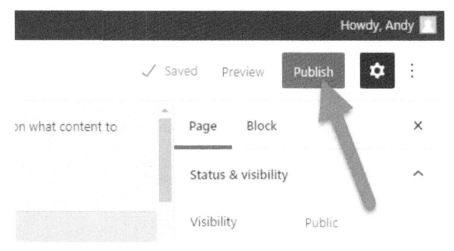

You will be asked to confirm you want to publish it, so click the second **Publish** button.

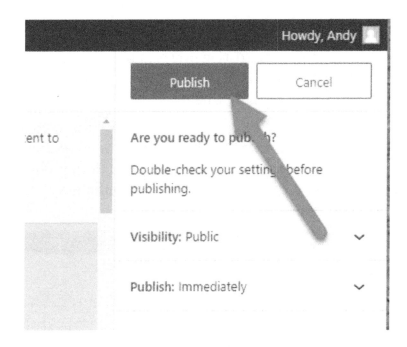

As soon as your Privacy Policy is published, go back to the Privacy settings page and make sure your new privacy policy is selected:

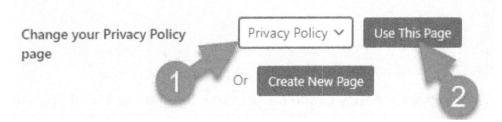

Click the **Use This Page** button.

This chapter has hopefully given you a better understanding of the **Settings** menu, how it is organized, and what the important settings do.

Congratulations!

Tasks to Complete

Go through each of the items inside the settings menu and make the changes described in this chapter.

RSS Feeds

We mentioned RSS feeds earlier when setting up the Reading options.

RSS feeds are an important part of your WordPress website, so I wanted to spend a little more time on this.

RSS stands for **R**eally **S**imple **S**yndication (or **R**ich **S**ite **S**ummary). An RSS feed lists information about the most recent posts on your site. This information is typically the title of the post (which links to the article on your website) and a description of it, which can be short or the entire piece.

The RSS feed is an XML document that would be difficult to read without special software, but XML is the perfect "language" to store this information.

Here is what raw XML looks like from one of my sites:

```
<?xml version="1.0" encoding="UTF-8"?><rss
version="2.0"
xmlns:content="http://purl.org/rss/1.0/modules/content/"
xmlns:wfw="http://wellformedweb.org/CommentAPI/"
xmlns:dc="http://purl.org/dc/elements/1.1/"
xmlns:atom="http://www.w3.org/2005/Atom"
xmlns:sy="http://purl.org/rss/1.0/modules/syndication/"
xmlns:slash="http://purl.org/rss/1.0/modules/slash/"
><channel><title>ezSEONews</title> <atom:link href="https://ezseonews.com/feed/" rel="self" type="application/rss+xml" />
<link>https://ezseonews.com</link> <description>Internet Marketing Tips &#38; Advice</description> <lastBuildDate>Tue, 15 Dec
2020 14:41:48 +0000</lastBuildDate> <language>en-US</language> <sy:updatePeriod> hourly </sy:updatePeriod>
<sy:updateFrequency> 1 </sy:updateFrequency> <generator>https://wordpress.org/?v=5.6</generator><image>
<url>https://ezseonews.com/wp-content/uploads/2019/01/cropped-favicon-32x32.png</url><title>ezSEONews</title>
<link>https://ezseonews.com</link> <width>32</width> <height>32</height> </image> <item><title>How to Add Audio Files and
Create Unique Playlists in WordPress</title><link>https://ezseonews.com/wordpress/how-to-add-audio-files-and-create-unique-
playlists-in-wordpress/</link> <comments>https://ezseonews.com/wordpress/how-to-add-audio-files-and-create-unique-playlists-
in-wordpress/#respond</comments> <dc:creator><![CDATA[Andy Williams]]></dc:creator> <pubDate>Tue, 15 Dec 2020 14:41:48
+0000</pubDate> <category><![CDATA[WordPress]]></category> <guid
isPermaLink="false">http://ezseonews.com/?p=7638</guid><description><![CDATA[<p>Keep your WordPress website or blog fresh and
memorable with audio files and playlists. This guide shows you how to add audio and create visitor-friendly playlists in easy
steps.</p><p>The post <a
rel="nofollow" href="https://ezseonews.com/wordpress/how-to-add-audio-files-and-create-unique-playlists-in-wordpress/">How to
Add Audio Files and Create Unique Playlists in WordPress</a> appeared first on <a
rel="nofollow" href="https://ezseonews.com">ezSEONews</a>.</p> ]]></description>
<wfw:commentRss>https://ezseonews.com/wordpress/how-to-add-audio-files-and-create-unique-playlists-in-
wordpress/feed/</wfw:commentRss> <slash:comments>0</slash:comments> </item> <item><title>What Is a Theme Framework in
WordPress?</title><link>https://ezseonews.com/wordpress/what-is-a-theme-framework-in-wordpress/</link>
<comments>https://ezseonews.com/wordpress/what-is-a-theme-framework-in-wordpress/#respond</comments> <dc:creator><![CDATA[Andy
Williams]]></dc:creator> <pubDate>Mon, 14 Dec 2020 13:24:37 +0000</pubDate> <category><![CDATA[WordPress]]></category> <guid
isPermaLink="false">http://ezseonews.com/?p=7629</guid><description><![CDATA[<p>Learn the basics of a WordPress theme
framework and why so many developers choose them. This piece is a must-read if you want to save money and time creating custom
WP themes.</p><p>The post <a
rel="nofollow" href="https://ezseonews.com/wordpress/what-is-a-theme-framework-in-wordpress/">What Is a Theme Framework in
WordPress?</a> appeared first on <a
rel="nofollow" href="https://ezseonews.com">ezSEONews</a>.</p> ]]></description>
<wfw:commentRss>https://ezseonews.com/wordpress/what-is-a-theme-framework-in-wordpress/feed/</wfw:commentRss>
<slash:comments>0</slash:comments> </item> <item><title>What Is an Attachment in WordPress?</title>
<link>https://ezseonews.com/wordpress/what-is-an-attachment-in-wordpress/</link>
<comments>https://ezseonews.com/wordpress/what-is-an-attachment-in-wordpress/#respond</comments> <dc:creator><![CDATA[Andy
```

RSS feeds provide an easy way for people to follow the information they are interested in. The raw XML isn't much use, but feed reader software can "translate" this into:

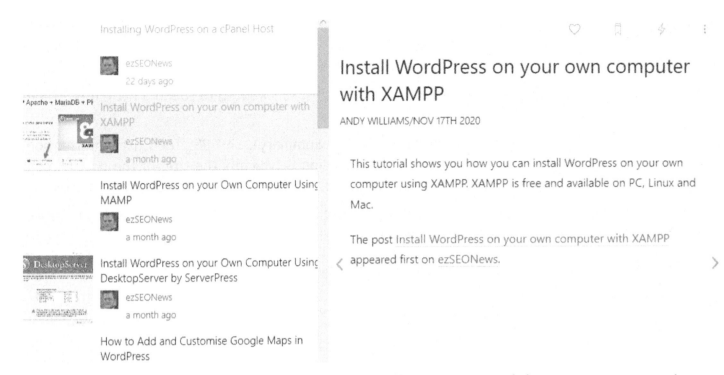

On the left pane is a list of posts found in the feed. Clicking on one of those opens up a preview on the right with the details found in the feed. In this case, the title, author, date, and an excerpt.

If someone was interested in following my site, they could subscribe to the RSS feed in an RSS feed reader and get notified of all new posts.

If you want to try a good feed reader, look for Feedly. There is a free version as well as a more comprehensive paid plan. Using a tool like Feedly, you can follow dozens of RSS feeds. RSS used this way allows you to scan hundreds of articles by title and description and only click through to read the ones that you are really interested in.

That is why we have RSS feeds on our site.

WordPress Has Multiple RSS Feeds

WordPress has the main RSS feed at **mydomain.com/feed**. Type that into your web browser, substituting mydomain.com for your real domain name, and you'll see yours. However, WordPress also creates a lot of other RSS feeds.

Remember earlier? We looked at how WordPress created some web pages to help organize your posts? These included category pages, tag pages, author pages, and so on. These types of pages are called "archive" pages because they list (or archive) multiple relevant posts. Each archive page has its own RSS feed, created by WordPress, to list all posts within that archive.

For example, an RSS feed is created for each category page on your site. If you have a category called "roses," then there will be an RSS feed showing just the posts in the roses category.

To find the URL of any category page feed, simply go to the category page on the site and add "**/feed**" to the end of it, like this:

```
←  →  C  ⌂   🔒 ezseonews.com/category/courses/feed/                                          ☆

⠿ Apps

<?xml version="1.0" encoding="UTF-8"?><rss
version="2.0"
xmlns:content="http://purl.org/rss/1.0/modules/content/"
xmlns:wfw="http://wellformedweb.org/CommentAPI/"
xmlns:dc="http://purl.org/dc/elements/1.1/"
xmlns:atom="http://www.w3.org/2005/Atom"
xmlns:sy="http://purl.org/rss/1.0/modules/syndication/"
xmlns:slash="http://purl.org/rss/1.0/modules/slash/"
><channel><title>Courses &#8211; ezSEONews</title> <atom:link href="https://ezseonews.com/categ
type="application/rss+xml" /><link>https://ezseonews.com</link> <description>Internet Marketing
<lastBuildDate>Thu, 03 Sep 2020 12:01:25 +0000</lastBuildDate> <language>en-US</language> <sy:u
<sy:updateFrequency> 1 </sy:updateFrequency> <generator>https://wordpress.org/?v=5.6</generator
content/uploads/2019/01/cropped-favicon-32x32.png</url><title>Courses &#8211; ezSEONews</title>
<width>32</width> <height>32</height> </image> <item><title>WordPress Essentials Course</title>
<link>https://ezseonews.com/courses/wordpress-essentials-course/</link> <dc:creator><![CDATA[An
<pubDate>Fri, 11 Sep 2020 13:30:00 +0000</pubDate> <category><![CDATA[Courses]]></category> <gu
isPermaLink="false">http://ezseonews.com/?p=7220</guid><description><![CDATA[<p>How to Use Word
builders by the hand. It saves time, money, and gives new users the confidence to work effectiv
environment </p><p>The post <a
```

Other RSS feeds created by WordPress include RSS feeds for tag pages, author pages, comments, search results, and so on. You can read more about WordPress RSS feeds here if you're interested:

https://wordpress.org/support/article/wordpress-feeds/

RSS Feeds Can Help Pages Get Indexed

RSS feeds contain links to the most recent posts on our website. We can use that fact to help our content get found more quickly by the search engines. To do this, we simply need to submit the RSS feed to an RSS directory, like Feedage.com.

Search Google for **RSS feed submission,** and you'll find more sites where you can submit your main feed. I recommend only submitting it to 3 or 4 of the top RSS feed directories, though.

When you publish new posts on your site, the feeds on your site are updated, which in turn updates the feed on the RSS directories. These directories now contain a link back to your new article. The search engines monitor sites like this to find new content, so your new article is found very quickly.

Posts Only

As I said earlier, RSS feeds show the most recent posts on your site. The emphasis is on the word **posts**, as feeds only include WordPress posts, not pages. This is an important consideration when you are deciding whether to add content as a post or a page. Do you need that content in the RSS feed for your site?

Here is an example. Acme, Inc has a business website, where most of the web pages are created using WordPress pages. They want to start publishing announcements about product releases, business news, etc. Should they use posts or pages for these announcements?

The smartest decision would be to set up a blog, using WordPress posts for all of the announcements. That way, journalists, customers, and anyone interested in following the news coming out from Acme, Inc., could subscribe to the feed and get the company announcements delivered directly to them.

The additional benefit is that as the RSS feed is updated with all of the new posts, any RSS submission site where that RSS feed was submitted will also be updated. Acme, Inc. will be getting new links from these feeds sites, and that can only mean the posts will get indexed quicker in Google. Google might even add these posts to the Google news section.

None of this would happen if company announcements were made using WordPress pages.

Later in the book, we will consider the structures of a site and how best to use posts and pages. A business site is one we will look at, so you'll see how to set that up inside WordPress.

Tasks to Complete

1. Go and have a look at Feedly.com and signup for a free account. Subscribe to some feeds that are of interest and look through them to find articles that appeal to you. This will give you a good idea of how feeds can be helpful.

2. Since you currently have no posts on your site, you won't have any meaningful feeds. Once you have some published posts, go and find the various feed URLs (main feed, category feed, tag feed, author feed & search feed).

User Profile

When someone comes to your website, they often want to see who is behind the information. Your user profile in WordPress allows you to tell your visitors a little bit about yourself.

In the Dashboard, hover your mouse over **Users** in the navigation menu and then select **Profile**. Alternatively, you can hover your mouse over the "Howdy, Yourname" in the admin bar at the top of the screen and click on your name or **Edit Profile**.

Another way of accessing your profile is to click the **Users** item in the menu, and you'll be taken to the **All Users** screen, where you will see a list of all users:

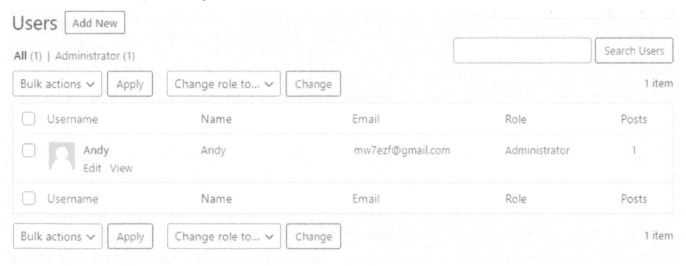

Click on your username to be taken to the user profile settings.

Your user profile will load.

At the top of the Profile screen, you'll see a couple of settings:

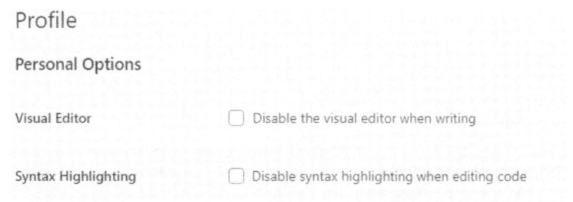

Leave these both unchecked, as they disable useful features of the Dashboard. Under these options, you can change the color scheme of the Dashboard if you don't like the default.

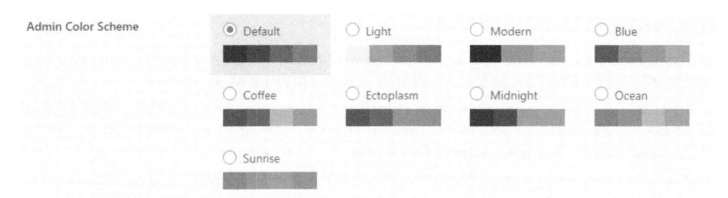

As you check an option, your Dashboard color scheme will change to reflect your choice. You may be spending a lot of time in your Dashboard, so choose a color scheme you like.

We then have these two options:

Keyboard Shortcuts	☐ Enable keyboard shortcuts for comment moderation. <u>More information</u>
Toolbar	☑ Show Toolbar when viewing site

I don't use keyboard shortcuts for comment moderation, but if you'd like to, enable the option and follow the "More Information" link to learn how to use it.

Show Toolbar when viewing site is an important option and should be checked. This will add an admin bar across the top of your website when you are viewing it while logged into the dashboard.

We will look at that later.

Under this, you have a dropdown box that allows you to change the language of your Dashboard. This is the language in the Dashboard only, not on your site. It was introduced so you can have the front end of your site in one language, and the dashboard administered in another. If you try changing this setting, check out the "Howdy Youname" menu top right. You can see it above in US English, but if I change my dashboard to UK English, this is what it looks like:

The next set of Profile options are for your name:

Name

Username	Andy	✖ Usernames cannot be changed.
First Name	Andy	✖
Last Name	Williams	✖
Nickname (required)	Andy	✖
Display name publicly as	Andy ˅	
	Andy	
Contact Info	Williams	
	Andy Williams	
	Williams Andy	

Your username cannot be changed. It will be whatever you chose when you installed WordPress.

Tip: If you really want to change your username, the easiest way to do this is just create a new admin user using the username you want. Log out of the dashboard and back in with the new user. Then delete the old user. You can assign any posts and pages created by the old user to the new one.

Enter your real first and last name (or your persona if you are working with a pen name).

For the nickname, you can write anything. I typically use my first name.

The **Display name publicly** field is populated with names built from the personal information entered on this screen.

Whatever you choose will be the name used on each page of your website telling the visitors who wrote the article:

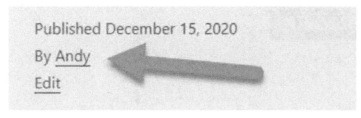

With most themes, including Twenty Twenty-One, the name links to the author page, which shows all articles written by that author. Incidentally, that author page also has its own RSS feed.

Try it!

Add "**/feed**" to the end of the author page URL, and you should see the XML code of the RSS feed.

The next few options are for contact information.

The only one that is required here is the email address, and we have talked earlier about how important that is. If you want to fill out the website field, you can, but this is more useful if you have multiple authors on your site, each with their own personal website.

Next in the profile is your **Biographical Info**.

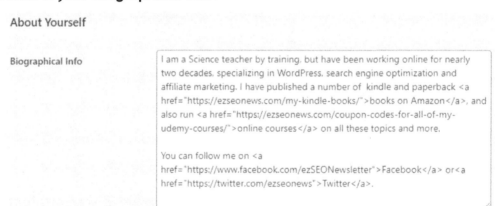

I recommend you fill in a short biography as some themes (including Twenty Twenty-One will show this at the top of the author page:

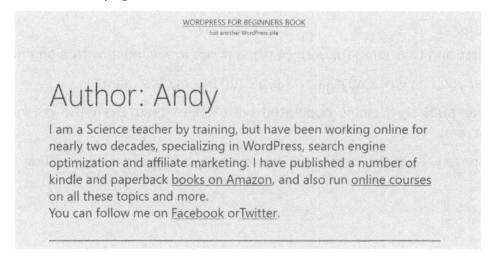

The Profile picture can be added by setting up a Gravatar.

Profile Picture

You can change your profile picture on Gravatar.

This is just an image linked to your email address. The photo will then appear on your author page and on any website where you leave a comment using that email address. We'll set this up in a moment.

At the bottom of the User Profile screen, you have an **Account Management** section.

Account Management

New Password

Set New Password

Sessions

Log Out Everywhere Else

Did you lose your phone or leave your account logged in at a public computer? You can log out everywhere else, and stay logged in here.

The first button allows you to generate a secure password to use with your account. If you are using a weak password, click the **Generate Password** button, copy the new password for your records, and then click the Update Profile link at the bottom.

The other tool in this section is a security measure that allows you to log out of WordPress everywhere except "here." Imagine your laptop was stolen, and you hadn't logged out of your Dashboard. The **Log Out Everywhere Else** button has your back. Click that, and the only place you will remain logged in is the computer you were at when you clicked the button.

A moment ago, we talked about Gravatars, so let's set that up now.

Gravatars

A Gravatar is simply a photograph or image that you can connect to your email address.

Sites that use Gravatar information, like WordPress, will show that image whenever possible if you contribute something.

For example, your photo will show on your author page. It will also show on any WordPress site where you leave a comment (assuming you use that photo-linked email address when leaving the comment). Some themes can even show your photo after each post, along with your author's bio.

Here is the box that appears after every post of mine on the ezseonews.com website:

Andy Williams

I am a Science teacher by training, but have been working online for nearly two decades, specializing in WordPress, search engine optimization and affiliate marketing. I have published a number of kindle and paperback books on Amazon, and also run online courses on all these topics and more. You can follow me on Facebook or Twitter.

OK, let's set up the Gravatar.

Go over to Gravatar.com and find the button or link to sign up or "Create your own Gravatar.".

You'll be asked to fill in your email address, pick a username, and choose a password. Note that this username and password is nothing to do with your WordPress site. This is a unique username and password for use on the Gravatar site.

Follow the on-screen instructions.

Gravatar.com will send an email to your email address. You need to open it and click the confirmation link to activate your new Gravatar account.

On clicking that link, you'll be taken back to a confirmation page telling you that your WordPress.com account has been activated. You can then start using Gravatar by clicking the Sign in button.

When you log in, you will then be taken to a screen that allows you to assign a photo to your email address. However, you don't have any images yet:

Just click the link, and you'll be able to choose an image from a number of different places, including upload, from a URL, or from a webcam.

Once you've selected your image, you'll get an option to crop it.

You now need to rate your image (remember, we mentioned Gravatar ratings earlier when setting up WordPress):

Choose a rating for your Gravatar

Site owners are given the option to choose how mature a gravatar may be before allowing it to appear on their site. Set a rating of more than G if your gravatar may not be suited for younger or sensitive audiences.

○ **rated G** This gravatar is suitable for display on all websites with any audience type.

○ **rated PG** This gravatar may contain rude gestures, provocatively dressed individuals, the lesser swear words, or mild violence.

○ **rated R** This gravatar may contain such things as harsh profanity, intense violence, nudity, or hard drug use.

○ **rated X** This gravatar may contain hardcore sexual imagery or extremely disturbing violence.

Set Rating

Just click the appropriate button.

That's it. Your Gravatar should now be attached to your site's email address. Whenever you leave comments on a WordPress site, use that email address, and your image will show up along with your comment (assuming they haven't turned Avatars off).

At the bottom of the **User Profile**, you'll see an **Application Passwords** section. This feature was introduced in WordPress 5.6 and helps authenticate requests that are made by third party tools, to various WordPress APIs. It's beyond the scope of this book, but if you ever need increased security, e.g., when handling XML-RPC requests, know this option is here.

Tasks to Complete

1. Go and claim your Gravatar.

2. Log in to your WordPress site and complete your user profile.

Find a WordPress site in your niche and leave a relevant comment making sure to use the same email address you registered for a Gravatar. Watch as your image appears next to your comment.

Tools

The next main menu is called Tools, and it has six options:

The **Available Tools** screen simply tells you how to convert your categories to tags or vice versa.

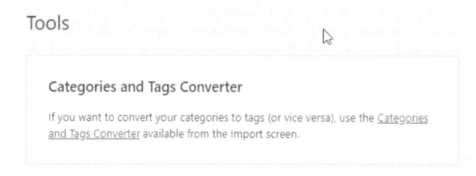

Clicking on the link will take you to a screen that lists a number of different tools, including the Categories and Tags Converter. If you want to use this or any other plugin on the import screen, I suggest you read the **Details** for the plugin by clicking the link under the plugin title.

The next option in the **Tools** menu is **Import**. This takes you to the same screen we've just seen. The import plugin is the last one on the list. Install it, and you'll then be able to "Run Importer" to import posts that you have previously exported from another WordPress site.

We probably should have covered the **Export** tool before the import tool. The Export feature allows you to export content from your site in a format that can be easily imported into another WordPress site. I used these features when I wanted to merge two or more websites into one larger website. Let's see the process.

To export content, click the **Export** menu:

Export

When you click the button below WordPress will create an XML file for you to save to your computer.

This format, which we call WordPress eXtended RSS or WXR, will contain your posts, pages, comments, custom fields, categories, and tags.

Once you've saved the download file, you can use the Import function in another WordPress installation to import the content from this site.

Choose what to export

(•) All content

This will contain all of your posts, pages, comments, custom fields, terms, navigation menus, and custom posts.

( ) Posts

( ) Pages

( ) Media

[Download Export File]

You can choose to export all the site content, posts, pages, or media files.

If you select posts, you will be given more options, including categories to export, export by author, date range, or status (published, scheduled, draft, etc.).

Once you have made your selection, click the export button to download the export file to your computer. This file will be an XML file (remember those?), with all the information required to re-create your content.

To import the content into another website, install the WordPress Import plugin we saw previously.

Once installed, the link under the plugin changes to **Run Importer**.

WordPress

Run Importer | Details

Import posts, pages, comments, custom fiel·
export file.

Click the **Run Importer** link, and you can choose the file to import.

With the file selected, click **Upload file and import**.

You will then have the chance to assign the content you are importing to a new or existing user:

Import WordPress

Assign Authors

To make it simpler for you to edit and save the imported content, you may want to reassign the

If a new user is created by WordPress, a new password will be randomly generated and the new

1. Import author: Andy (Andy)

   or create new user with login name: [Andy   ]

   or assign posts to an existing user: [- Select -   ∨]

Import Attachments

☐ Download and import file attachments

[Submit]

If you have images or other media in the exported content, check that box **Download and import file attachments** to make sure everything comes across.

When you click the **Submit** button, the content will be imported.

The next menu is for **Site Health**.

At the top, under the heading, you'll get an overall rating.

Site Health

◯ Good

Status   Info

Mine says **Good**.

There are then two tabs. Once for status and one for info.

The status tab gives you important information about your WordPress installation. As you can see from the screenshot below, mine has two suggestions.

Site Health Status

The site health check shows critical information about your WordPress configuration and items that require your attention.

2 recommended improvements

Your site is running an older version of PHP (7.3.25)	Performance	∨
A scheduled event is late	Performance	∨

Passed tests ∨

The first one is telling me that I am using an older version of PHP. PHP is the software on my web hosting server that makes it possible for WordPress to run. It is important that you keep this up to date so that all features of WordPress, themes, and plugins can work securely and without issue. You should be able to update PHP in your hosting cPanel, but if you have any problem doing that, talk with your hosting support, and I am sure they will do that for you.

Do your best to fix any security issues that arise here.

Under these recommendations, you should be able to see a drop-down box that lists all of the tests that your installation passed. This is just for information, but you might like to look through that list.

If you need to contact WordPress or your host about issues you are having, click on the **info** tab, and copy the site info to the clipboard.

Site Health

Results are still loading...

Status   Info

Site Health Info

This page can show you every detail about the configuration of your WordPress website. For any improvements that could be made, see the Site Health Status page.

If you want to export a handy list of all the information on this page, you can use the button below to copy it to the clipboard. You can then paste it in a text file and save it to your device, or paste it in an email exchange with a support engineer or theme/plugin developer for example.

Copy site info to clipboard

You can then paste the text into a support email to send.

The next Tools submenu is **Export Personal Data**. This can be used to export a zip file containing the data that has been collected about a user on your site. This will help you comply with privacy laws if a user requests a copy of the data you have about them.

The **Erase Personal Data** will allow you to delete a user's personal data upon verified request. This deletion is permanent and cannot be reversed. If a user ever requests their personal data is deleted, this is the tool for you.

Appearance Menu

The **Appearance** menu contains these items:

This menu, as the name suggests, gives you access to settings that control the appearance of your site.

Clicking on the Appearance menu opens the themes page where you should have just one theme installed:

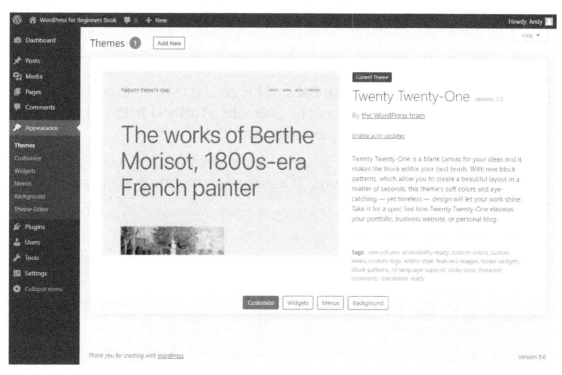

At the top of the themes screen, you have the option to **Add New** theme, which will search the WordPress theme repository for approved (and therefore generally safe) themes that you can install and use on your site. We've already seen how this works.

NOTE: You will often hear people referring to WordPress themes as templates. While the two things are not totally the same thing, people often use the words interchangeably to mean the same.

If you have more than one theme installed, you'll see a thumbnail of each theme and a search box at the top to help you search your installed themes. Since you only have one theme installed, you won't need the search feature on this page, so it is hidden.

Any thumbnails on this screen will have one or more buttons.

Which buttons are shown for a theme depends on the theme. These buttons take you to specific locations in the dashboard that you can also navigate via the menu on the left.

So the Customize button will take you to the Customize screen found in the Appearance menu. The Widgets button will take you to the Widgets screen, and the Menus button will take you to the Menus screen.

Usually, after installing a theme, I'll want to go to the Customize screen (a live editor) to make a few changes. I can either click that button or go to Customize in the Appearance menu.

Customize Live Editor

This is what it looks like for the Twenty Twenty-One theme:

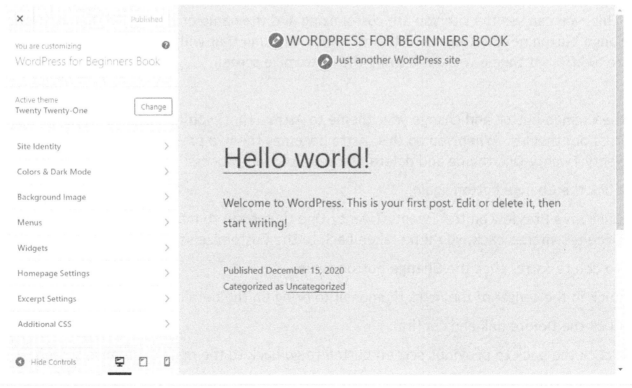

On the left is a menu that gives you access to site settings.

Most of these settings can also be found buried in the dashboard's **Settings** menu. The advantage of editing them here is you get to see a live preview when you do make changes. The live preview is the large window on the right.

The settings you see in the left menu will depend on the theme you have installed. If you are not using the Twenty Twenty-One them, your menu will look different from the one above.

At the top, you'll see something like this:

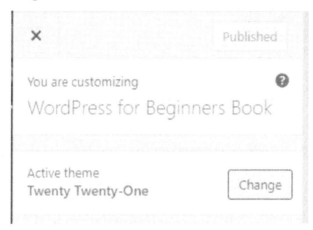

The X in the top left will close the Customize screen.

If you make any changes in the Customizer, the **Published** button will change to a **Publish** button, inviting you to click it to save your changes.

Under this, you can see the site you are customizing and the name of the active theme. Notice the **Change** button next to the active theme name. Clicking that will allow you to install and activate a different theme without leaving the Customize screen.

Try it.

Click the **Change** button and change your theme to Astra. Hint, you'll find that in the wordpress.org themes. When you do this, Astra becomes the live preview theme. To go back to the Twenty Twenty-One theme and delete Astra, follow this process:

1. Click the **Change** button again.

2. Click **Live Preview** on the Twenty Twenty-One thumbnail to make it the "live preview." Once it switches back, you'll be taken back to the Customize screen.

3. To delete Astra, click the **Change** button again.

4. Click in the center of the Astra thumbnail to bring up the details page.

5. Click the **Delete** link and confirm.

Now click the **back to previous screen** button to go back to the main Customize screen:

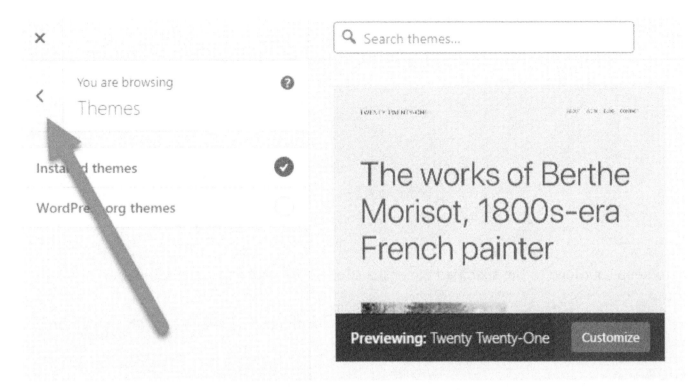

You then have a number of menu items. Remember that what you see in this menu is controlled by your theme, so if you have other entries, they are specific to your theme:

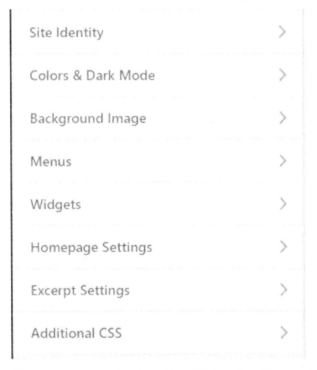

Site Identity – This section allows you to edit the Site Title, Tagline, add a logo and a site icon.

Note: To add a logo, you click the **Select Logo** button, which will open a screen that tells you how big the logo should be:

Drop files to upload

or

Select Files

Maximum upload file size: 300 MB.

Suggested image dimensions: 300 by 100 pixels.

Try to keep your logo to the specified dimensions, or at the very least, the same ratio of height to width.

The site icon is commonly called a Favicon. It is the small icon you see in the tab on your browser when you visit your site:

The images you use for these should be a perfect square and at least 512 x 512 pixels in dimension.

Colors & Dark Mode – This is a setting to adjust the background color of your site to a "dark mode" if a visitor requests it. Find out more details on that by clicking on the option and following the link to the support article.

Background Image – Inserts an image on the background of your site.

Menus – Create, edit, and manipulate menus from within the customize screen.

Widgets – Handle widgets without leaving the customize screen. Click on that now.

On the left, you'll see a welcome message the first time you go there. Read it, then click the **Got it** button so you can view the add widget panel.

You can add widget bocks directly on this screen by clicking that add button and selecting what you want to insert.

Try it. Click the + button and add a heading to the widget area.

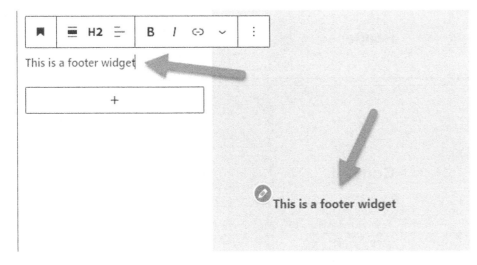

Scroll down the preview window so you can see the footer area of your site. You should see the heading you just added in the footer area.

Try adding a few more blocks.

When you are done, you can delete these blocks by selecting them, clicking on the **Options** menu, and selecting **Remove Block**.

Homepage Settings – This allows you to specify what you want on your homepage: the latest posts or a static page.

Excerpt Settings – On archive pages, do you want the full text displayed or a summary?

Additional CSS – If you want to tweak the design on your site using CSS, this option allows you to add custom CSS without having to edit CSS files. The advantage of adding custom CSS in this way is that it won't be overwritten if your theme updates itself. CSS is beyond the scope of this book.

As you have seen, most of these menu items will allow you to manipulate site settings without leaving the customize screen. The added bonus is that the changes you make are visible in the live preview.

If you do make changes, make sure you click the **Publish** button at the top to save them. Then exit the **Customize** screen using the X in the top left corner. You'll be taken back to the Dashboard.

The next item in the **Appearance** menu is **Widgets**.

Widgets

Widgets allow you to easily add visual and interactive components to your site without needing any technical knowledge. It's one of the things that makes WordPress so powerful.

If you want to add a list of your latest posts, there's a widget for that. Perhaps you want to add a poll to your site? That can be done with widgets too. There are some widgets specifically designed for these (and other) purposes, but you can also create your own using any of the blocks built into Gutenberg.

When a designer creates a WordPress theme, their initial drawing will probably have "widgetized" blocks drawn onto it so they can visualize which areas will accept widgets. Maybe it will look something like this (with the shaded areas able to accept the widgets):

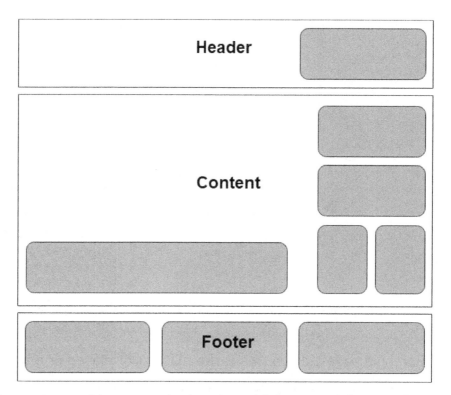

The usual areas that accept widgets are the header, sidebars, and footer. Sometimes you can also add widgets after post content.

With the Twenty Twenty-One theme, we have already seen that the only widgetized area is the Footer.

Let's have a play around with widgets. Click **Widgets** in the menu to be taken to the widgets screen. First time you do this, you'll get a welcome message, so just read through that and we can get started.

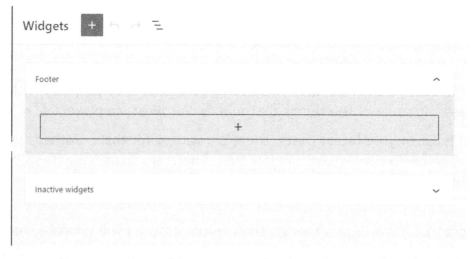

We saw this screen earlier, so no need to go over the interface again. Let's just try out a few widgets.

Click on the **Add Block** button in the toolbar.

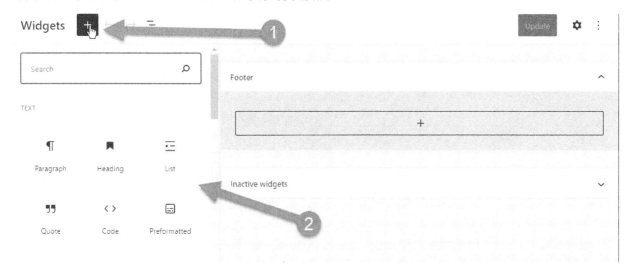

The panel on the left opens to show you available blocks and widgets you can insert.

The blocks are divided into related groups, so you have text blocks, media blocks, etc. These are the same blocks that are available to you as you create your posts or pages. At the top is a search box, so you can easily search for the widget you want to insert if you know what it's called.

You will also see a group called **Widgets**. These are blocks that have been created specifically to be used as a widget and they have specific functions.

For example, the **Latest Posts** widget will add a list of the most recent posts on your site. The **Navigation Menu** widget will insert one of the menus you created into the widget areas, and so on. The **Search** widget will insert a search box, and so on.

Close the block panel on the left by clicking into in the empty space underneath the **Inactive widgets** section in the preview area.

Now click on the + inside the box in the **Footer** area:

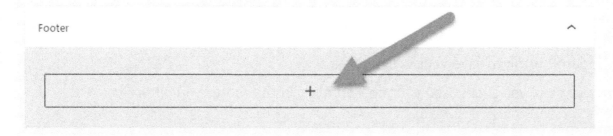

The same block panel opens as a popup screen. If you click **Browse All**, the popup closes and the larger panel on the left opens again.

Open the popup panel again and click on **Heading** block in the block panel. This will insert that block into the **Footer**. Give it the title **Welcome** and make it as Heading 2 by using the formatting menu above the Heading block.

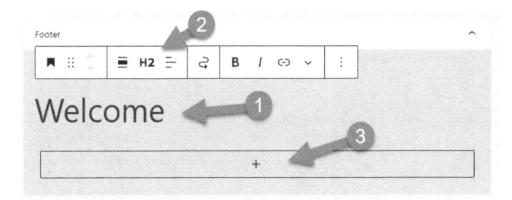

Now click the + underneath he heading to open the popup panel again and add a paragraph block. Add something like:

"We hope you find what you are looking for, but if not, please use the search button below:"

Now click the + underneath he paragraph block and insert that search widget we saw earlier. Hint: You can find it by browsing all blocks, or by using the search feature built into the popup panel.

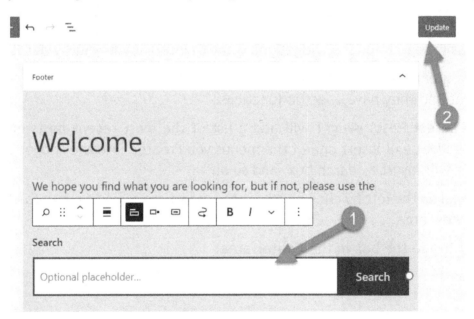

Now click the **Update** button to save your widget area.

If you now visit your site, you should see your new content in the footer widget area:

Hmmm. That's not exactly what I wanted. I'd prefer the title to be on top of the paragraph and the search box underneath. The good news is that it's easy to fix using **Groups**.

Go back to the **Widgets** screen and select the heading block.

Holding the SHIFT key on your keyboard, click on the paragraph and the search box, so all three are selected.

You'll see a menu appear above the blocks. Click the **Options** button and select **Group**.

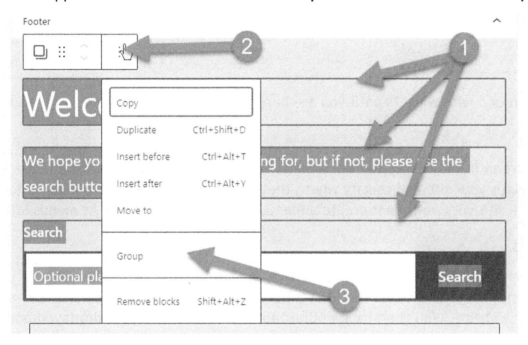

The three blocks have now been grouped into a single widget. You can see this by clicking on the **List View** button:

See how the three blocks are now indented under the **Group**?

Click **Update** to save your widget settings and go back and visit your homepage.

Welcome

We hope you find what you are looking for, but if not, please use the search button below:

Search

[   ] [Search]

Have a play around with widgets until you are happy manipulating the blocks and grouping them.

Menus

The **Menus** screen inside the **Appearance** menu takes you to a screen that will allow you to build menu systems for your site and specify where they go in your site design. Since we don't have any content on the site yet, we cannot create a menu. Therefore, we'll look at menus later.

Background

This menu was added by the Twenty Twenty-One theme, and clicking on it will take you back into the **Background** Image section of the **Customize** screen. From there, you can add a background image to your website. You then have options about how that image is displayed and mirrored in the background. Try it.

The Theme Editor Menu

The bottom item in the **Appearance** menu is the **Theme Editor**. This allows you to edit the theme's PHP files. This is an advanced topic requiring programming skills, so we won't be covering it here.

Tasks to Complete

1. Go to the Customize screen and go through all the option screens to familiarize yourself with them.

2. Go and explore the widget area. Add some widgets to your site, and then view the site in your browser to see what they do and how they format the information.

3. Practice grouping blocks so they behave as a single widget.

4. Try building a widget with a photograph of yourself and a brief bio linking to your Facebook page.

Plugins

In this section, we are revisiting plugins in a little more detail.

We'll look at what plugins are, where you can get them, and how to install them. I'll also walk you through the installation and configuration of a few important plugins.

In the Dashboard sidebar, you'll see the **Plugins** menu:

The menu has three options:

Installed Plugins – To view the current list of installed plugins.

Add New – To add a new plugin. You can also access the **Add New** screen via an "Add New" button on the **Installed Plugin** screen.

Plugin Editor – This is a text editor that allows you to modify the PHP code of the plugins. We won't be looking at this advanced topic.

Click on the installed plugins menu to go to the plugins screen. This is what mine looks like on the blank site I have been using in this book:

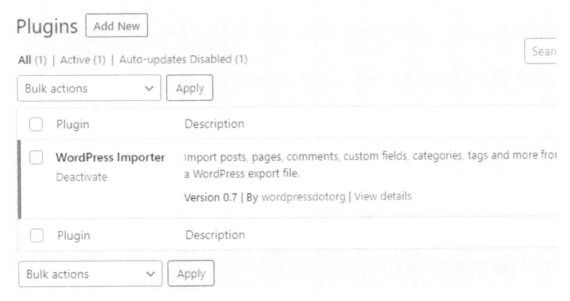

I have one plugin installed. It's the WordPress Importer plugin we looked at earlier.

Across the top of the table, you'll recognize the filter links. What you see in this filter menu will depend on the plugins you have installed. For example, here is that same menu on an established site of mine:

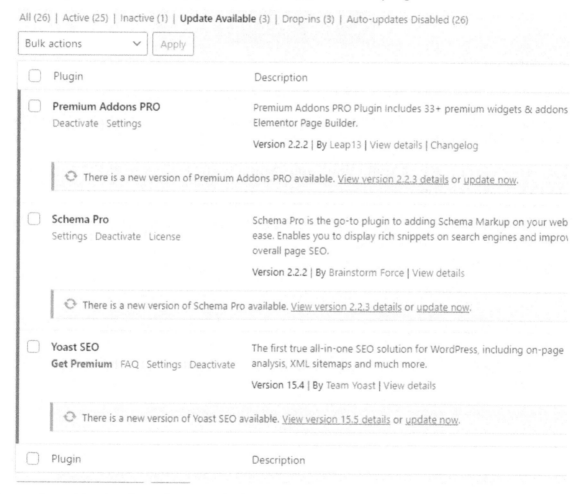

Remember that these links are filters. If I wanted to see the three plugins that need updating, I could click the **Update Available (3)** link to display just those plugins:

You will see that this site has plugins labeled as Drop-Ins. These are special types of plugins that alter core WordPress functionality.

You may see other filters. For example, if you have deactivated a plugin that was once active, you might also see another group called **Recently Active**. See (1) below:

To activate a plugin is easy. Just click the **Activate** link underneath the name of the plugin (2).

Deactivating is just as easy. The **Deactivate** link is present for all active plugins.

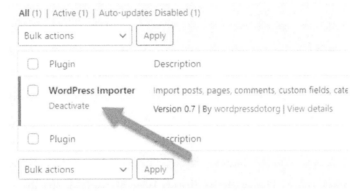

When you add new plugins or activate/deactivate plugins, the filter menu at the top will change to reflect the changes.

Deleting Plugins

We did this earlier when we cleared out the pre-installed stuff. But let's go through it again.

To delete a plugin, it needs to be inactive. If you have an active plugin you want to delete, first deactivate it.

To delete a plugin, click the **Delete** link under the plugin name (the delete link only appears on inactive plugins):

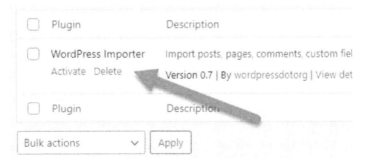

You will be asked to confirm the deletion, so click OK. The plugin and all its files will be removed from your server.

If you have more than one plugin to delete, there is a quicker way to remove multiple plugins in one go.

Make sure the ones you want to delete are deactivated, then check the box next to each plugin you want to delete:

Now select **Delete** from the **Bulk Actions** drop-down box and click apply:

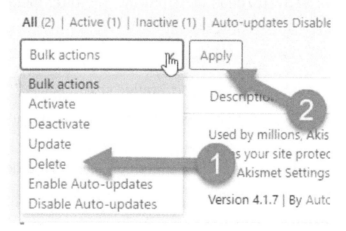

You will be asked to confirm that you really do want to delete all selected plugins.

NOTE: The bulk action drop-down box also allows you to activate, deactivate, update, and enable/disable auto-updates on the plugins.

Plugins that Modify Menus

Some plugins may add their own menu items, like this one:

This upgrade link takes you to a website to buy an upgraded version of the plugin.

But the plugin also added its own menu in the sidebar:

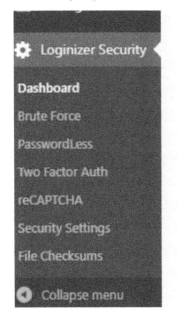

Since plugins (and themes) are created by third-party programmers, these types of extra menu items are quite common.

Installing Important Plugins

Before we look at the plugins, I need to let you know that plugins are updated frequently, and their appearance may change a little. However, these changes are usually minor cosmetic changes, so if you don't see exactly what I am showing you in these screenshots, look around. The options will be there somewhere.

I'll be installing what I consider essential plugins that add must-have features to any site. However, for each plugin I install, there are plenty of alternatives. If you decide that you don't want to use one of the plugins I am installing because you have an alternative you prefer, that is fine.

Let's go ahead and install a few very important plugins, then configure them.

UpdraftPlus

Backing up anything on a computer should be a priority. While good web hosts do keep backups for you, if your site gets infected with any kind of malicious code and you don't find out about it for a while, all their backups could be infected.

I always recommend you have your own backup plan, and fortunately, there is a great plugin that can help.

Click the **Add New** item in the **Plugins** menu.

Search for **Updraft.**

Find and install this plugin:

After clicking the **Install Now** button, the installation process will proceed. Once complete, this button changes to say **Activate**. Click to activate the plugin.

You'll have a new **UpdraftPlus Backups** section in the settings menu.

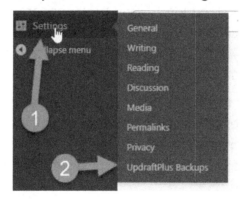

Click on it to access the settings of this plugin.

You can take manual backups on the **Backup/Restore** tab:

More powerful still is the ability to schedule automatic backups of your site. To do that, click on the **Settings** tab.

Choose a frequency and the number of backups to retain.

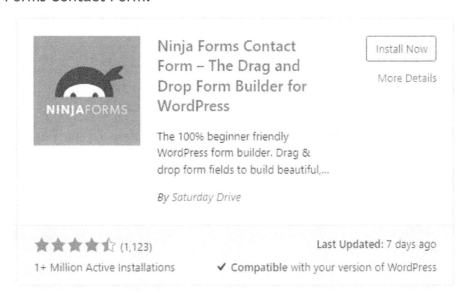

Now scroll down and click **Save Changes** at the bottom.

You will notice that on this screen, you also have the option of using remote storage for your backups. If you have a Dropbox account, that is a great place to send backups. They'll be off your server and safe if you ever need them. You can also get backups emailed to you, though full backups can be very large.

I won't go into details on setting this up. Just follow the instructions that are included with the plugin.

Ninja Forms Contact Form

It's important that site visitors can contact you, so let's install a contact form plugin.

It's called Ninja Forms Contact Form.

Install and activate the plugin.

This will add a new menu called **Ninja Forms** in the sidebar of the Dashboard.

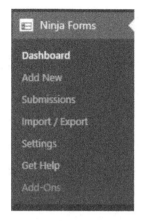

If you click on **Ninja Forms**, you'll be taken to the plugin's dashboard, where you can see that the plugin created a contact form for you.

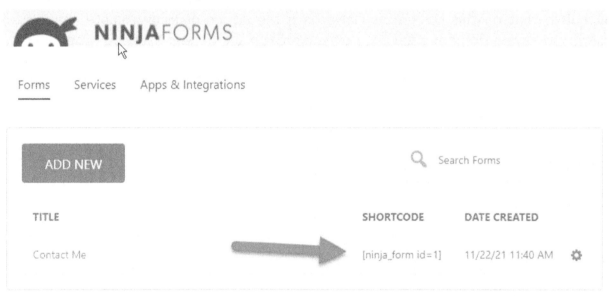

We will use this one, as it is a perfectly good contact form. You just need to copy the **Shortcode**. You can see the shortcode in the table above. It's [ninja_form id=1].

Once you have copied it, create a new page by clicking on **Add New** in the **Pages** menu.

Add a title for the page, e.g., Contact Form, Contact, or Contact Us.

Now click the + button next to the text "Start writing or typing...."

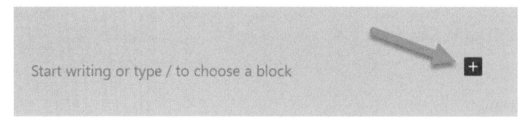

In the popup that appears, type **short**, and select shortcode from the search results:

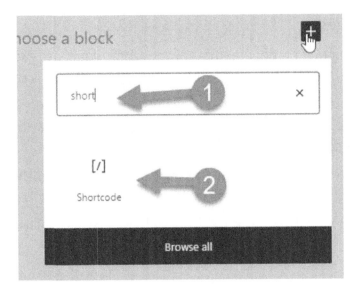

Paste the shortcode you copied from Ninja Forms into the box:

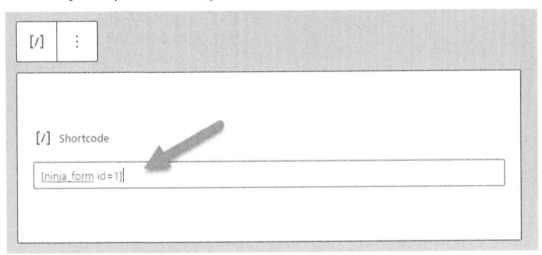

Publish the page using the publish button top right. You'll also need to click the second publish button that appears.

Once the page is published, a message comes up at the bottom to let you know. There is also a link to view the page. Click it:

When the page opens, you will see the contact form.

WP-Insert for "Legal Pages"

The legal pages are the important documents you need on your site from a legal point of view. We've already seen the Privacy Policy earlier, but others include Terms of Service, Disclaimer, etc.

Ideally, you would want a lawyer to draw these up for you because no plugin is going to be 100% complete or take your personal needs into account. There are also web services out there where you can buy packs of legal documents you can update and use.

So, with that said, be aware that while I will show you a plugin to add these to your site, it is only to get you up and running quickly. I'd still recommend you get proper legal documents drawn up.

There are a few plugins out there that can create quick legal pages. The one I suggest you look at is called WP-Insert.

Install and activate it.

You'll find a new menu in the sidebar navigation labeled **Wp Insert**. Click on it to open the settings.

Now, this plugin does a lot more than just generate legal pages. It's also a full-blown ad manager, which is useful if you want to put adverts or AdSense on your site.

For legal pages, we need to scroll down to the "Legal Pages" section:

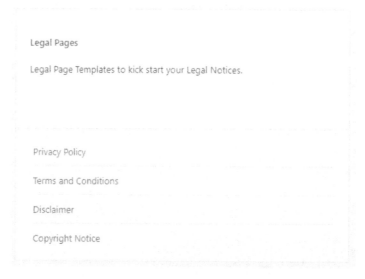

You can see that this plugin can create a Privacy Policy (which you should have created earlier, so probably don't need), Terms and Conditions, Disclaimer, and Copyright Notice. You create all these pages in the same way, so I'll just go through one with you.

Click on the **Terms and Conditions** link.

A dialogue box pops up with the information you need to read.

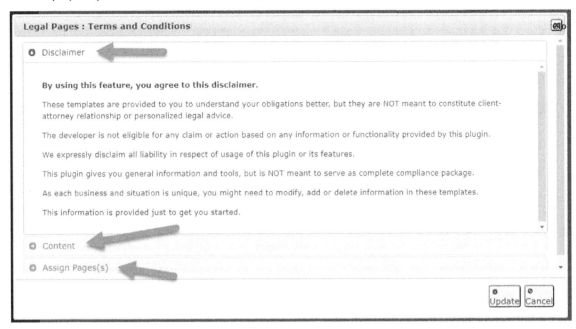

Notice that the plugin recommends you get proper legal advice for this type of document. That echoes the advice I gave you earlier.

Note the three tabs on the left: Disclaimer, Content, and Assign Page(s).

Click on the **Content** tab. You will see the default content of the Terms and Conditions page. You can edit this if you want.

Now click on the **Assign Page(s)** tab.

Click the **Click to Generate** button.

The plugin will create a page for the document. Once done, you can see it selected in the **Assign a Page** box:

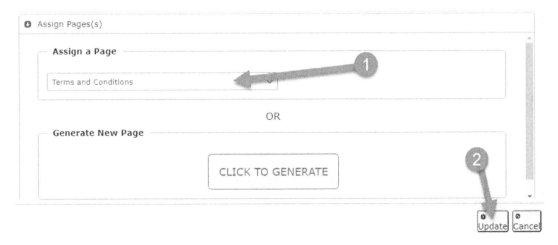

To confirm this is correct, click the **Update** button.

If you click on the **Pages** link in the sidebar navigation to view all of your pages, you will now find the Terms and Conditions page.

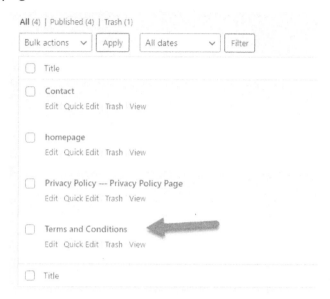

Click on the **View** link to open the page in your web browser.

Repeat for other legal documents you want to create.

Yoast SEO

Go to **Add New** plugin and search for **Yoast SEO.**

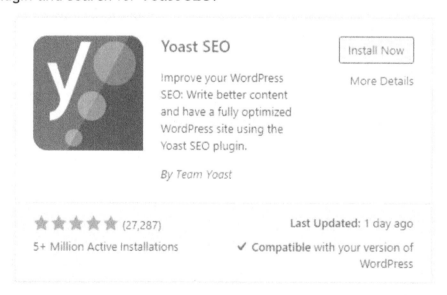

Install and activate the plugin.

This plugin installs a new menu in the sidebar called **SEO.**

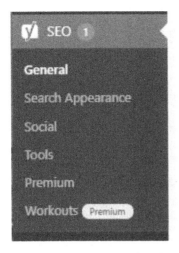

Click on the **General** link in the SEO menu.

Across the top, you'll see some tabs – Dashboard, Features, Integrations, and Webmaster Tools.

Click on the **Features** tab to see a list of features you can enable and disable. Currently, all of them (except usage tracking and premium features) are enabled by default. I am not going to go through what each of these does, but I will tell you that I disable SEO Analysis and Readability analysis because I don't find them very useful. While SEO analysis is a nice idea, it does focus on single keyword optimization (in the free Yoast SEO plugin), which is something I stay away from. Google hates content that is highly optimized around a single keyword, so paying too much attention to this feature can only get you into trouble, in my humble opinion.

One option that I do want to highlight is the XML sitemap feature. Click on the "?" icon next to this feature to open a little more information and a link to your own sitemap.

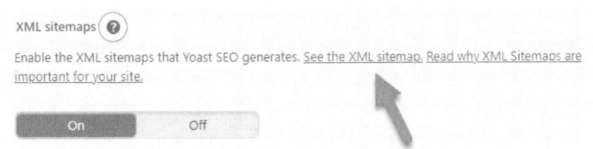

If you click on the link to **See the XML Sitemap**, it should open in a new window:

XML Sitemap

Generated by YoastSEO, this is an XML Sitemap, meant for consumption by search engines.

You can find more information about XML sitemaps on sitemaps.org.

This XML Sitemap Index file contains 3 sitemaps.

Sitemap	Last Modified
https://andyjwilliams.co.uk/post-sitemap.xml	2020-09-15 12:21 +00:00
https://andyjwilliams.co.uk/page-sitemap.xml	2020-12-09 11:58 +00:00
https://andyjwilliams.co.uk/category-sitemap.xml	2020-09-15 12:21 +00:00

Only content that has been published will show on the sitemap, so what you see will depend on the stage of development your site is at. If the sitemap is empty, you probably don't have any content published. If you have published content but don't see the sitemap, then make sure:

1. WordPress is installed on an online web host and not on your own computer (an advanced technique some developers use). The sitemap feature won't work in some local environments.

2. You have published posts or pages. Note that a draft post is not a published post. 😊

3. Yoast SEO settings have been saved to ensure the feature is enabled.

4. If it still doesn't show anything, go to the **Permalinks** section (inside the **Settings** menu of the sidebar navigation) and just scroll to the bottom to save the permalink structure.

The sitemap should now appear.

Now click back on the **Dashboard** tab at the top of the General Yoast SEO settings.

You'll see a box that says **First-time SEO configuration**.

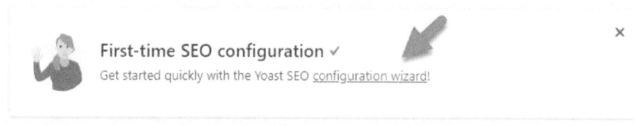

In the box is a link to the configuration wizard. Click the link.

You'll be taken through a multi-step procedure to configure the plugin.

I won't go through the wizard here as it changes a lot, and by the time you read this, it may already look different. Just follow along and answer the questions as you go.

If you are unsure of any answers, just accept the default setting.

The last screen of the wizard is promotional, so don't be lured into buying something you don't need □.

By the time you have finished the wizard, the plugin will have made some necessary changes to your WordPress install, even adding in something called "structured data" for your posts and pages. Structured data is beyond the scope of this book, but essentially it gives Google extra information that can be used to create rich snippets in the search results. If you want to learn more about structured data, please see my course on the subject. A link to all of my courses can be found in the Resource section at the end of this book.

OK, click on **Search Appearance** in the SEO menu.

Across the top, you can see several tabs:

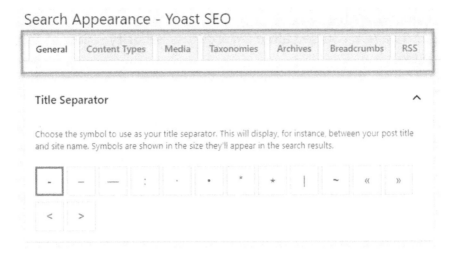

The tabs across the top set up how the different types of content are displayed on your site and in the search results. Have a look through the settings but leave everything with the default values.

Finally, click on the **Social** link in the SEO sidebar menu. This is where you can go in and add/edit the social media links you want to associate with the website.

OK, for now, we are done with the Yoast SEO plugin.

WordPress Security

I would recommend you check out a free plugin called All in One WP Security.

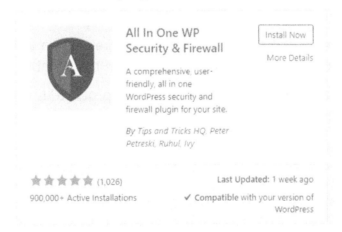

It is a great way to secure your WordPress website from hackers. I'll warn you that the plugin is quite complicated and can lock you out of the Dashboard if you set it up too aggressively. I, therefore, won't be covering it in this book. I simply don't want readers to face problems and then have no one to ask for help.

If you want to see a video tutorial I created for the basic (and fairly safe) setup of this plugin, you can watch it here:

https://ezseonews.com/secureit

If you want a more comprehensive look at WordPress Security, including a more detailed set of tutorials for this plugin, I have a course called "WordPress Security – How to Stop Hackers." There is a link on that web page.

Akismet Anti-Spam

WordPress may install Akismet by default. It is an excellent anti-spam plugin that is free for non-commercial sites. However, if you have a commercial site, the plugin does require you to pay for a commercial license.

When you activate the plugin, you'll see a banner in your dashboard asking you to set up an account:

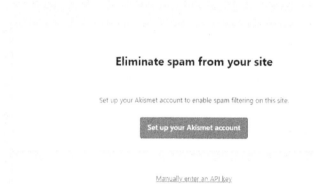

Click the **Set up your Akismet account** button.

A screen opens that has a list of the different plans available. When you sign up for one, you'll be given an **API key**. You can use that to activate your copy in the dashboard.

You will see a few options, but essentially your site is now protected from spam by Akismet.

If you wanted a free alternative, I would go with Stop Spammers:

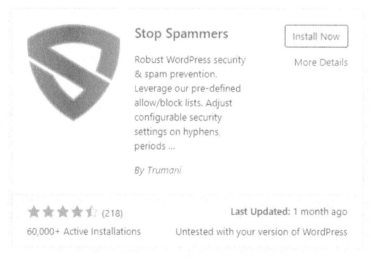

It has a lot of features giving you fine control over the protection of your site, but also does the basic spam blocking exceedingly well. Simply installing and activating it will give you basic protection.

OK, those are the essential plugins installed. It's time to complete some tasks.

Tasks to Complete

1. Install Updraft Plus and set it up.

2. Create a contact form using Ninja Forms.

3. Install WP-Insert and create the "legal" pages.

4. Install Yoast SEO and run through the wizard to set it up.

5. Check your sitemap is working (except local installs).

6. Consider installing and configuring the All-In-One Security plugin.

7. Activate Akismet if you want to use it and get your API key. Otherwise, investigate Stop Spammers.

Comments

I mentioned earlier that a lot of people turn comments off because they can't be bothered with comment moderation. The way I see it, comments are the life and soul of a website and help to keep visitors engaged with you and your content. You need to offer visitors this chance to connect with you. Therefore, you really should keep comments turned on.

We have already configured the "discussion" settings to blacklist comments with known spam content (using the blacklist you found by searching on Google), and that will cut down on comment spam considerably. However, there are dedicated anti-spam plugins available as well.

If you are running a non-commercial website, I recommend you use Akismet. It is probably the best anti-spam plugin available. It is for non-commercial use only, though, and commercial sites need to pay for it.

I am reluctant to recommend a free comment spam plugin because most of the ones I have tried did not work effectively. Stop Spammers is one of the better ones and works well with the All-In-One Security plugin I recommended earlier in the book. The All In One plugin does include some great anti-spam features as well, so do investigate those. You will find them in the **Spam Prevention** menu within the main **WP Security** menu of the plugin.

Moderating Comments

When people comment, their comments won't go live until you approve them. This is how we set the site up earlier. If you had comments set on auto-approve, you'd most likely find so many spam comments on your site that you'd be pulling your hair out. Manual approval is the only way to go, and it does not have to take a long time.

Let's see how easy it is to moderate comments.

If you click on **Comments** in the sidebar, you are taken to the comments section.

Across the top is a menu with All, Mine, Pending, Approved, Spam & Trash:

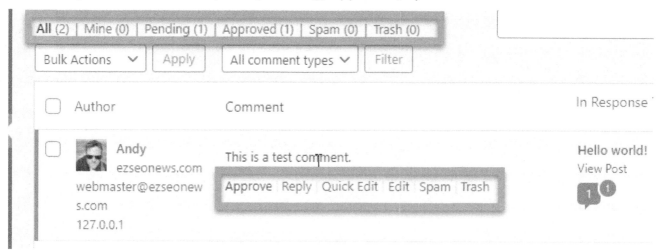

Below this, you can see a comment I added to the site. When I added the comment, I used an email address linked to a Gravatar. That's why my photo is there. When you leave a comment on a WordPress site, your photo will show up too if you use a Gravatar-linked email address.

If you hover your mouse over a comment in the list, a menu appears underneath that comment, which you can click to Approve, Reply, Quick Edit, Edit, Spam & Trash.

If the comment is OK, click the Approve link. If the comment is clearly not spam, but you don't want to approve it, then click on **Bin**. If the comment is spam, click the spam link.

NOTE: Remember the **WP All-In-One Security** plugin? It has a nice feature that will automatically block comments from the IP addresses of comments in the spam folder. You'll find that by using this feature, you can improve spam recognition and make your job of moderation easier.

You can also edit comments if you want to remove something (like a link) or correct a spelling error from an otherwise good comment.

I recommend you don't reply to comments until you approve them. My typical workflow is this:

1. Moderate comments.
2. Go to the Approved comments by clicking the Approved link at the top.
3. Reply to comments that need a reply.
4. Go to the **Bin** and empty it.

In the screenshot above, you will see a (0) next to the spam link. That means there are no spam comments. However, if you have any, click on the spam link to see what the spam folder contains.

You can see the comment and author for each comment in the list. If you decide that a comment is not spam, mouseover it and click **Not Spam** from the menu. The comment will be sent to the **Pending** pile and await moderation.

You also have the option to **Delete Permanently**. To delete all spam in the spam folder, you can simply click the **Empty Spam** button at the bottom. When you do delete spam, it is permanently removed.

The **Bin** holds all comments that were sent to the "trash." Like the Spam folder, you can retrieve comments that are in the Bin (if you need to) using the mouseover menu.

Finally, we have the **Approved** list. These are all comments on your site that have been approved. Click the link in the menu at the top to view them.

All comments in the Approved list have a mouseover menu as well, allowing you to **reply** to the comment if you want to. You can, of course, change your mind about an "approved comment" and send it to spam or trash if you want to, or even **Unapprove** it if you want to think about it.

What Kinds of Comments Should you Send to Spam/Bin?

You will get a lot of comments that say things like "nice blog" or "Great job." I suggest you trash all comments like this because they are spam comments. Their only purpose is to try and get a backlink from your site to theirs through flattery.

I recommend you only approve comments that:

1. Add something to the main article, either with more information, opinions, or constructive information. That means never approving a comment that could have been written without that person ever reading your post. Comments MUST add something to your content. If they don't, I suggest you send them to the Trash.

2. Never approve a comment where the person has used a keyword phrase for their name. You'll see people using things like "best Viagra online" or "buy XYZ online" as their name. No matter how good the comment is, trash it. What many spammers do is copy a paragraph from a good webpage on another website and use that as their comment. The comment looks great, but the name gives away the fact that the comment is spam.

3. I would suggest you never approve trackbacks or pingbacks. Most will not be real anyway.

With comments, be vigilant and don't allow poor comments onto your site as they will reflect badly on both you and your website.

Here are three spammy comments left on one of my websites. All three would go straight to spam without hesitation:

Author	Comment
roof cleaning ct youtube.com/watch? v=UXHr0i7l3_A ramiro_scorfield@bigstring.com 104.168.49.137	Very good written story. It will be helpful to anyone who usess it, as well as me. Keep doing what you are doing – i will definitely read more posts.
legendary wars Hack Tool facebook.com/LegendaryWarsCheatsHackToolAndroidiOS jeseniahertzog@live.com 5.34.246.202	Post writing is also a fun, if you be familiar with then you can write if not it is complicated to write.
Marriage Ceremony Tips By Joe Whoisology.com terigiorza@googlemail.com 23.232.165.73	Good info. Lucky me I discovered your blog by chance (stumbleupon). I have book-marked it for later! Approve Reply Quick Edit Edit Spam Trash 📋 ✋ Report to SFS

These comments are totally irrelevant to the content they are commenting on. You'll get a lot of comments like this. Spammers seem to think that a bit of flattery is all that is required to get a comment approved.

Also, check out the names of the "people" leaving each comment.

Tasks to Complete

1. Install an anti-spam plugin if you want to use one, or look into the anti-spam features of the All-In-One Security plugin and enable those.

2. Whenever there are comments on your site, moderate them. Spam or Trash any comments that are not "adding to the conversation."

Media Library

Media includes things like images and videos that you want to use in posts, as well as other downloads you want to offer your visitors, e.g., PDF files.

The media library is a convenient storage area for all such items.

You can go and have a look at your Media Library by clicking on **Library** in the **Media** menu. All items are shown as a thumbnail. Clicking on a thumbnail will open the **Attachment Details** screen, which shows you the media item, URL, Title, etc. You even have some basic editing features if you need to crop, scale, or rotate an image.

Uploading stuff to your media library is really very easy.

You will usually add media directly from the **Add Post** screen when typing a piece of content. However, if, for example, you have a lot of images that you want to upload at any one time, it is often quicker to do it directly in the Media library.

How to Upload New Media

Click on **Add New** in the **Media** menu, or, on the **Media Library** page, click the **Add New** button at the top.

Uploading media is as simple as dragging and dropping into the dashed box:

(You can also click the **Select Files** button and select them directly from your hard disk.)

Note that there will be an upload limit that is stated under the dashed box. This tells you the maximum size of uploads on your server. Mine is 300MB. Yours may be different. If you need something bigger, you need to talk with your web host about it as they need to change settings within your hosting package.

To drag and drop something, open the file manager on your computer. Select the file(s) you want to upload and click and hold the left mouse button on the selected items. Now move your mouse, dragging the items to the dashed box in the Media Library screen. You can then release the mouse button, dropping those files into the Media Library.

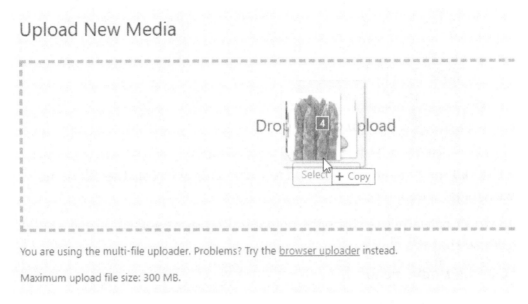

NOTE: You may see something a little different when you drag your images over the box. In the screenshot above, I entered the "Upload Media" screen by clicking on the **Add New** link in the Media menu. However, if you clicked on the **Library** menu item first and then clicked the **Add New** button, things are a little different. Try it and see.

When you drop images in the dashed rectangle, they are uploaded to the library. When the upload is complete, you'll be shown a list of uploaded images:

Clicking the Edit link to the right of this thumbnail to open the **Edit Media** screen. This screen allows you to add a caption, ALT text, and description for the "attachment" page that is created for your image.

To access the actual attachment page created, click the permalink at the top of this screen:

Have a look at the URL of that attachment page. The URL will use the filename of the image to construct the web page's filename.

Chances are you won't actually use this page on your site unless you run some kind of image/photo site. However, know that it's there.

Click on **Library** in the **Media** menu.

You should see your uploaded images:

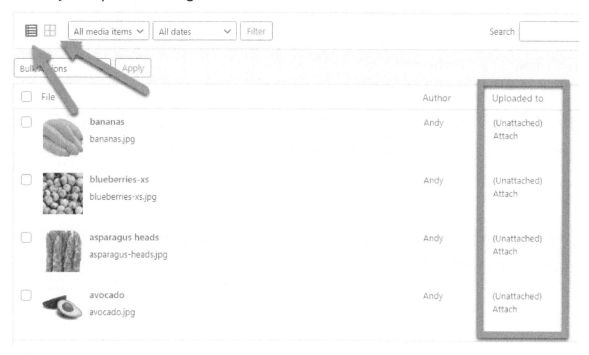

What you see depends on which view you have selected. See those two icons top left? Click on each one to see what they do.

In the screenshot above, you can see that the images I uploaded are not "attached." An unattached image means it is not being used on any post or page. We will look at how to add an image (or video) to a post later in this book. But for now, just try uploading a few images to get the hang of things.

NOTE: The media library is there to provide a central location for all of the media files you want to use on your site. This is not limited to images. You can upload other file formats like PDF, MP4, etc. However, there are some file formats that WordPress will not let you upload for security reasons. PHP files are one example. If you want to upload a file to offer as a download on your site, but it is not accepted for upload, then zip it up and upload the zipped file instead.

At the top of the media library screen, you'll see some filtering options:

Help ▾

Media Library | Add New |

▤ ⊞ | All media items ⌄ | | All dates ⌄ | | Bulk select | Search | |

The exact filtering options are different on the Grid and List views, so look at that. The screenshot above is the grid view.

The two drop-down boxes allow you to view only a specific type of media, e.g., images, or only those media items that were uploaded in a particular month.

We've already looked at the first two buttons that change the view of your uploaded media. Select that first button to show the table view.

When viewing your media library in the "list view," each item has the now-familiar mouse-over menu, which allows you to **Edit**, **Delete Permanently**, or **View,** that media item.

There is a column showing you the date the item was added to your library.

Note that columns in the media library are sortable by clicking the title of the column.

Mouse over a column header to see an "ascending/descending" arrow and click to re-order.

If there are columns you don't use and don't want to see, you can hide them by using the screen options. Remember those?

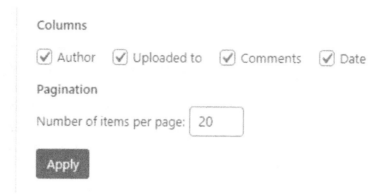

Columns

☑ Author   ☑ Uploaded to   ☑ Comments   ☑ Date

Pagination

Number of items per page: 20

Apply

Just unclick whichever items you don't want to see. You can even specify how many media items you see per page in your library.

If you have a lot of media in your library, there is a handy search feature:

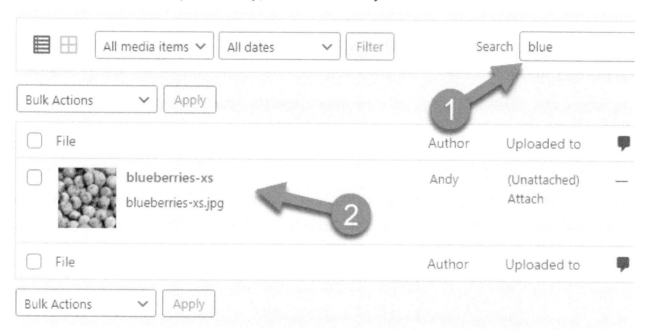

In the screenshot above, I entered blue and hit the return key. The results returned the one media item, including the word "blue." The search feature will look for your search text in both the title of the media and its description. If the word appears in either, it is shown in the search results.

To cancel the search filter, click on the "X" in the search box:

.. and press enter to refresh the results.

The media library also gives you **Bulk Actions** (something that can be applied to multiple items in one go).

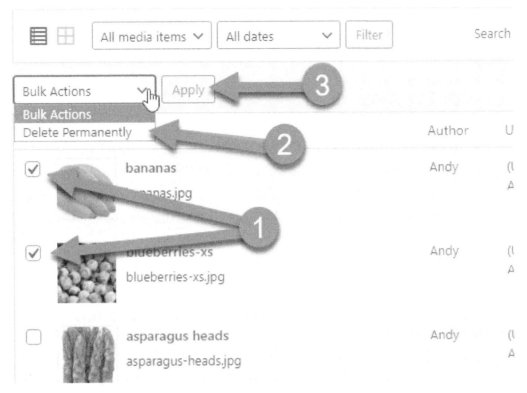

Next to each media item is a checkbox. If you want to delete several media items, you can check each one and then select **Delete Permanently** from the **Bulk Actions** drop-down box. Click **Apply** to delete the checked items.

That's it for the Media Library for now. We will come back to this when we look at how to add content to your site.

Tasks to Complete

1. Go and explore the media library. Practice uploading a photo, video, or sound file and grabbing the URL.

2. Try using the search feature to find a specific piece of media in your library.

Pages v posts

When you want to add written content to your site, you have two options. You can either create a **Page** or a **Post**. In terms of adding/editing, these two are very similar, but they are quite different in terms of function.

This may sound confusing to people who are new to WordPress (or maybe even new to website building). After all, isn't a post on your site a page? Doesn't a page on your site contain a post?

For some reason, WordPress creators decided to name these two types of content "posts" and "pages," and it does cause confusion. However, you do need to understand the basic differences between them when it comes to building your site.

Since WordPress was originally designed as a blogging platform (i.e., to help build websites that were constantly updated with posts about whatever was going on in that blogger's life), posts were designed for these regular, chronological updates.

Let's summarize these two types of content and then we'll dive a little deeper:

WordPress **posts** are *date-dependent, chronological, can be grouped into categories, and will appear in the RSS feeds of the site.*

Wordpress **pages** that are *date-independent (so not chronological), are not designed to be grouped, and do not appear in the site's RSS feed.*

Clearly these two types of content were designed for different purposes.

Posts were originally designed to be ordered by date. A post you created yesterday should logically appear lower down the page than a post you make today. Newer posts are inserted at the top of the page, and older posts are pushed off the bottom. If you think back to the WordPress reading settings, we saw that the default homepage of a WordPress site shows posts in this manner.

A typical blog will be structured this way. Let's look at an example.

Suppose you were keeping a blog about your weight loss program. On day one, you weighed in at 210lb, so you write about that and what you have done for the day to help with your diet. Each day you write a new entry as a kind of personal journey on your weight loss progress.

When someone comes to your site, they see the daily posts in chronological order. This means visitors to your 'blog' can follow your story logically and see how your diet is working out for you.

This type of chronology is not possible with pages (well, it is, but it takes a lot of effort plus plugins to achieve, so why bother?). Pages do not have any defined order, though they can have a hierarchy of parent and child pages.

OK, so date-dependency is one important difference between WordPress posts and pages. What else?

Well, posts can be categorized, pages cannot (at least not without plugins).

Suppose you were creating a site about exercise equipment. You might have a series of reviews on different treadmills, another set of reviews on exercise bikes, and so on.

Using posts allows us to categorize our content into relevant groups. If I had ten reviews of various weight loss programs, I could create a category on my site called weight loss programs and add all ten reviews to this category by writing them as posts.

Putting related content into the same category makes sense from a human visitor's point of view, but also from the point of view of a search engine. If someone were on your site reading a review of the Hollywood Diet, it would be easy to use features of WordPress posts to highlight other reviews in the same category. This can be done with posts on autopilot, but it is a much more manual process if you tried doing the same thing with pages.

Posts can also be tagged with related words and phrases.

Tags are an additional way to group and categorize your content. We'll discuss tags later, but for now, realize that they can be used to categorize your content further to help your visitors and the search engines make sense of your project.

It is possible to create tags for pages as well, but once again, only with plugins. As a rule, we try not to use plugins unless they are essential, as they can slow down the loading time of a website and possibly add security vulnerabilities if they are not well maintained by their creators.

Another great feature of posts is that they can have **Excerpts**. These are short descriptions of the article that can be used by themes and plugins to create a Meta description tag or a description of the article in a list of related articles. For example, below is a related posts section (created using a plugin) on one of my websites. It shows excerpts being used for the post descriptions:

Related Posts

1. What Are Tags in WordPress

   Learn about tags in WordPress, how they differ from Categories, and when to use them. Tags are a simple, highly-effective way for webmasters to organise and enhance web content.

2. How to Add Custom Hyperlinks to Your WordPress Gallery Images

   You can add custom links to your gallery or single images in WordPress. This step-by-step tutorial shows how to quickly add and edit custom links from the Post Edit screen.

3. How to Add WordPress Menu Items Without Linking to a Page

   A quick how-to Guide on how to add non-linking titles for Dropdown Menus in WordPress. Create neat menus for posts and pages to improve site navigation for your visitors.

Another important feature of posts is that they appear in your site's RSS feed. Remember, we talked about how important RSS feeds are earlier in the book. RSS feeds highlight the most recent posts, but pages are not included.

When to Use Posts and When to Use Pages

OK, this is the million-dollar question that I get asked a lot!

This will depend on the type of website you want to build. For a lot of company websites, using pages for most of the content makes sense, like this:

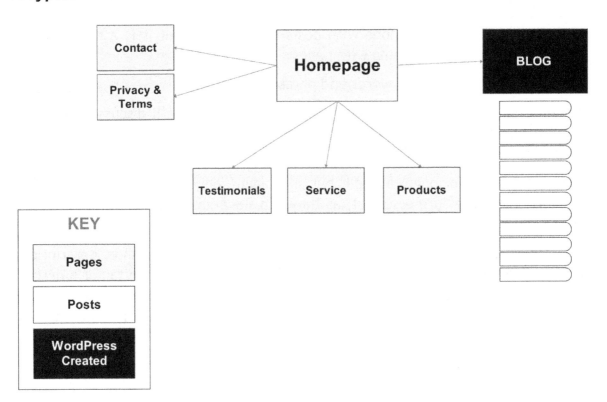

In this model, the company site uses WordPress "pages" for all the main important content that they want to convey to visitors. That includes Homepage, Contact, Privacy, Terms, Testimonials, Services, and Products. These pieces of content are all isolated and unrelated to one another. The date of publishing is not important, so they are date-independent, and they don't need to be on the company RSS feed.

The company site also has a blog, and in this model, the blog is built with posts. From the point of view of this company, what features of posts make them ideal for the company blog?

The fact that posts are chronological? Sure. That means the company can post product updates, with the latest announcements at the top! The fact that these blog posts will end up in the company RSS feed will help spread the news.

What about a site that is intended to be a blog? What would that look like?

I would suggest this model is ideal for a blog:

A Typical Blog

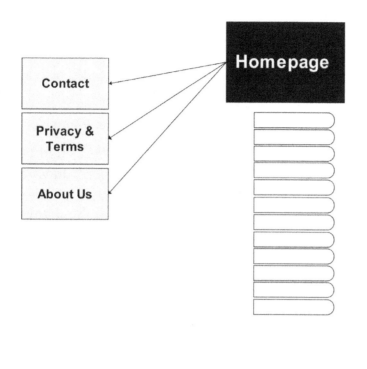

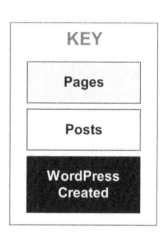

In this model, the homepage would be created by WordPress and just display the last ten or so blog posts. Newer posts would appear at the top, while older posts fall off the bottom (and on to page 2).

The blog posts would all use the power of WordPress "posts" (chronology and feed), while pages would only be used for Contact, Privacy, Terms, and an About Us page.

But WordPress has even more up its sleeves. The properties of posts, especially the ability to categorize posts, allow us to be very creative in site design. The main type of website I usually build is a completely different model to the two we've just seen. It uses elements of both a blog and a business site but throws categories into the mix. I call it a "Hybrid" model, and it is one that particularly suits niche sites, eCommerce, etc. It's a model that relies on the fact that a piece of content does not live on an island. It is related to other pieces of content, which can be grouped and categorized.

This model offers great SEO benefits as well as organizing content in a logical manner to help both visitors and search engines.

Before I show you the model, let me first distinguish between two types of content that a site like this typically has.

The first type of content is the stuff created for visitors. It's the content you want your visitors to see and share to social media, and Google to rank highly. We'll call this type of content, **Niche Content**. This will include articles, reviews, videos, infographics, etc., that **you create for your targeted audience**. These are the money pages!

The second type of content is the stuff that you need to have on the site, but from a financial point of view, you don't really care whether visitors find it. This type of content does not fit into logical groups. Typical examples would be a Privacy page and Terms of Service. I'd also add the "contact" page to this group. I call this type of content my "legal pages."

For my Hybrid model, the rule is to **Use Posts for "Niche Content" and Pages for "Legal Pages."**

The **Homepage** and **About Us** are exceptions to the types of content I described earlier. These are obviously important pages that we want our visitors to see, yet they don't have any features that would require a WordPress "post." They are not part of a group, are date-independent, and we don't need them in the RSS feed. Therefore, these pages are created using a WordPress Page.

Here is a diagram of the model:

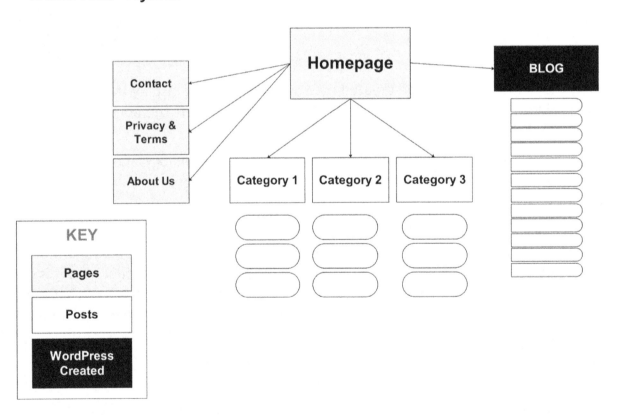

WordPress Pages have been used for Contact, Privacy, Terms, About Us & the Homepage.

The homepage has been created as a static page, which we will look at later in the book.

The site has several categories with posts grouped into those categories. There is also a separate blog for announcements or any other type of short communication you want to put together.

An example of a site that uses this model could be a niche site about Amateur Radios. The homepage might be an article explaining a little about the hobby and what makes it interesting. From the Homepage, you'd see links to the different manufacturers of amateur radio, so Kenwood, Icom & Yaesu. Clicking these links would take you to a category page for that manufacturer, listing all posts on the site that are in that category. The Homepage would also have a link to the site's blog, as well as all the "legal pages."

So those are the three models I will be taking further in this book. However, WordPress is so flexible that you might want to design your own structure. To help, in the next chapter, we are going to consider Categories and Tags in more detail. These are properties of WordPress "posts."

Tasks to Complete

1. Go over this section until the differences between pages and posts are clear in your mind.

2. Can you make a list of any legal pages you may require on your site?

3. Think about a local vacuum shop and draw out a website structure that would be a good design for that company. In the next chapter of the book, we'll use a vacuum shop as an example when thinking about categories and tags.

Categories & Tags

We have already touched on categories and tags earlier in the book, but let's have a closer look at them so you can fully understand what a powerful addition they are to your toolbox.

Both categories and tags are ways to categorize your posts.

All posts MUST be assigned to a category, but tags are optional. Categories are, therefore, more important than tags.

While WordPress allows you to put a post into several categories, I highly recommend that a post is only assigned to ONE category. If you think a post can fit equally into two or more categories, I suggest you are using the wrong categories.

Think of categories as the main way to organize your posts. Think of tags as an additional organizational tool that can be called upon if needed.

Let's consider a website about vacuum cleaners. What would your main categories?

If you had a bunch of vacuum cleaner reviews, how would you want them organized?

What about articles on how to repair different types of vacuum cleaners?

Possibly more importantly, how would your website visitors expect them to be organized? I like to think about what my visitors would want to search for at the site and use that as a starting point.

Here are a few things I believe visitors will search for:

- Dyson
- Handheld
- Dyson Ball
- Eureka
- Bagless
- Cordless
- Hoover
- Upright
- Canister
- Miele
- HEPA filter

Which of these should be categories?

If you used all of them as categories, what category would you assign an article about a handheld

Dyson vacuum? Dyson, or Handheld?

Clearly, we need to think about this.

Remember, I recommend a post is only assigned to one category. This gives your site a better, clearer structure and will help with SEO. Forcing yourself to think of one category per post can actually help you find the best categories for your site.

Of those ideas listed above, which ones would make the most sense if a vacuum could only be in one category?

How about "bagless"?

Nope. A vacuum could be bagless, upright, and a Dyson.

The obvious categories from that list would be the ones where a vacuum could only fit into one - the brand names. My categories would, therefore, be:

- Dyson
- Eureka
- Hoover
- Miele

A Dyson DC25 vacuum cleaner review could only go into one category - the Dyson category.

So, what about the other terms:

- Handheld
- Dyson Ball
- Bagless
- Cordless
- Upright
- Canister
- HEPA filter

A vacuum could be cordless, bagless, and contain a HEPA filter! That's a clear indication that these features are not suited as categories. However, they are perfect as tags!

For example, my review of the Dyson DC25 vacuum would be in the category Dyson but could be tagged with ball, HEPA, bagless & upright.

The beauty of using tags is that for every tag you use, WordPress will create a page just for that tag.

The tag page will list ALL posts that have been assigned that tag.

In the example above, WordPress would create FOUR tag pages. One for "ball," one for "HEPA," one for "Bagless" and one for "Upright."

The "HEPA" tag page will list all vacuums on the site that have been tagged with HEPA - it helps visitors find more HEPA vacuums if that is what they are interested in.

Using brand names for categories, and features as tags, a visitor can come to the site and find just about anything they want. If they know they want a Dyson, they can go to the Dyson category page and see a list of all Dyson vacuums. If they know they want a handheld vacuum, then they can go to the handheld tag page and see all handheld vacuums, no matter what brand they are.

Tags help search engines too. They provide additional information about an article, helping search engines understand what the content is about.

There is no doubt that tags are powerful. However, with that power comes some responsibility. If you abuse tags, your site will become spammy, and you'll struggle to get any traction in the search engines.

I have seen sites where posts have been tagged with 10, 20, 50, and even several hundred tags. Don't believe me? See this screenshot showing the tags for a post on one website I came across:

You don't need to be able to read the words in that screenshot to get the point. I've had to reduce the size of the screenshot to get all the tags into view. There are over 160 tags for that single post. I happen to know that Google penalized that site.

Every tag on that list will have its own tag page. Many of the tags were only used once on the entire site, so there were 100+ tag pages with just a single post listed as using that tag.

To think about this in another way, if a post lists 160 tags, and this is the only post on the website, then the site will contain over 160 pages. It'll contain one post, 160 tag pages, which are all nearly identical (as they all just list the same post), and a few other pages that WordPress creates for us, which will be almost identical to the 160 tag pages.

The way the webmaster used tags in this example is clearly spam, and search engines hate spam. Please, use tags responsibly!

Let's look at one more example.

Think of a recipe website about puddings, desserts, cakes, and so on.

You might have main categories like:

- Ice cream
- Cakes
- Muffins
- Mousse
- Cookies

These are the obvious categories since a dessert will only be able to fit into one of the categories. To further classify the recipes on the site, we'd use tags that would add a little more detail about each post.

What type of tags would you use?

Are you stuck for ideas? Think of the "features" of the desserts.

Tags usually choose themselves as you add more content to a website. For example, you might find that a lot of recipes use chocolate, or walnuts, or vanilla, or frosting (you get the idea). These would make perfect tags because a visitor with a hankering for chocolate could visit the chocolate tag page and see a list of all ice cream, cakes, muffins, mousse, and cookies that include chocolate.

Do you see how the tags help with additional layers of categorization? The tag pages become useful pages for visitors.

This is the mindset you are looking to develop as you utilize tags for your own website.

A Few Guidelines for Using Tags

1. Keep a list of tags you use on your site, and make sure you spell them correctly when you reuse them. Remember, if you misspell a tag, another tag page will be created for the misspelled version.

2. Don't create tags that will only apply to one post. Remember, tags are there to help classify your content into groups. Most tags will be used several times on a site, and their use will increase as you add more content. I'd recommend that you only use a tag if it will be used on three or more posts.

3. Only pick a small number of relevant tags per post. I'd recommend somewhere between three and six tags per post, but if some need more, then that's fine. If some need less, that's OK too. This is just a general rule of thumb.

4. NEVER use a tag that is also a category.

Setting Up Categories & Tags in Your Dashboard

Categories and tags are properties of posts, so you'll find the menus to work with them under the

Posts menu in the sidebar.

Categories and tags can either be set up before you start writing content or added as you are composing it. The most common method is to set up the main categories before you begin, but add tags while you are writing your post.

I recommend that you create a description for all tags and categories, and to do that, you will need to go into **Categories** editor and **Tags** editor using the Posts menu.

OK, let's go and set up a category first. Click on the **Categories** menu:

On the right, you will see a list of current categories.

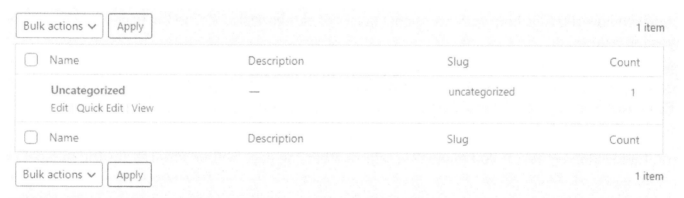

Deleting a category does not delete the posts in that category. Instead, posts that were only assigned to the deleted category are set to the default category Uncategorized. The default category cannot be deleted.

Categories can be selectively converted to tags using the category to tag converter.

There is only one category – Uncategorized. WordPress set this up for you during the WordPress installation. Since it is currently set as the default category for posts, it cannot be deleted. We could create another category and then make it the default for posts. We could then delete the Uncategorized category. However, we can just change the name of the uncategorized category, so it is useful for the site.

We can use **Quick Edit** in the menu underneath the category title to change the category name AND the category slug. The slug is just the text that is used in the URL to represent the category of the post. Remember we set up Permalinks earlier to look like this:

/%category%/%postname%/

The %category% variable is replaced by the category slug, and the %postname% variable will be replaced by the post name.

Click on **Quick Edit** and delete the word **Uncategorized** from the **Name** and **Slug** boxes.

Type your desired category name into the **Name** box, but leave the slug empty. While you can type in the slug as well, WordPress will create a default slug for you if you leave it blank.

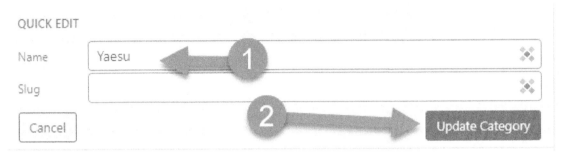

Click the **Update Category** button.

For the slug, WordPress uses the name you supplied but converts it to lowercase and replaces any spaces with dashes.

Therefore, a category name of **Amateur Radio** would have a default slug of **amateur-radio.**

If you want to edit the description of the category, you need to click the **Edit** link under the category title. That will take you to a screen with a text editor where you can type the description.

Try it. Click the **Edit** link and enter a description. When you are done, scroll to the bottom of the page and click the **Update** button.

Go back to the **Categories** screen by clicking categories in the Dashboard menu.

Adding A New Category

Let's create a new category.

On the left, there is space to enter a Name, Slug, and Description. Fill in these fields:

Add New Category

Name

Kenwood

The name is how it appears on your site.

Slug

The "slug" is the URL-friendly version of the name. It is usually all lowercase and contains only letters, numbers, and hyphens.

Parent Category

None ˅

Categories, unlike tags, can have a hierarchy. You might have a Jazz category, and under that have children categories for Bebop and Big Band. Totally optional.

Description

Kenwood Corporation is a Japanese company that designs, develops and markets a range of car audio, hi-fi home and personal audio, professional two-way radio communications equipment, and amateur radio equipment.

The description is not prominent by default; however, some themes may show it.

[Add New Category]

Now click on the **Add New Category** button.

The new category will be displayed in the category list:

Name	Description	Slug	Count
Kenwood Edit Quick Edit Delete View	Kenwood Corporation is a Japanese company that designs, develops and markets a range of car audio, hi-fi home and personal audio, professional two-way radio communications equipment, and amateur radio equipment.	kenwood	0
Yaesu Edit Quick Edit View	**Yaesu** is a Japanese brand of commercial and amateur radio equipment. It was founded as **Yaesu** Musen Co., Ltd. (八重洲無線株式会社, **Yaesu** Musen Kabushiki-gaisha) in 1959 by a Japanese radio amateur Sako Hasegawa with call sign JA1MP in the Tokyo neighborhood of **Yaesu**.	yaesu	1

When you were adding or editing a category, you might have seen an option to specify a parent category. I didn't mention it at the time, as there is no "parent" for my default category, but what is a parent category?

Parent Categories & Hierarchy

Categories can be hierarchical. In other words, you can have categories within categories.

An example might be a website about car maintenance. I might have a category called Toyota, but then want sub-categories called Yaris, Auris, Prius, Land Cruiser, for the different maintenance articles on each type of car.

Therefore, the parent category would be Toyota, and the child categories would be Yaris, Auris, Prius, Land Cruiser, etc.

To achieve this, I'd create the Toyota category first, then select it as the parent category when I created the subcategories.

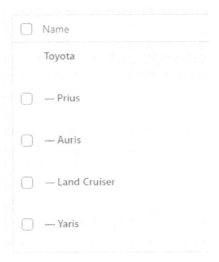

In the list of categories, you can spot parent/child relationships because the parent category is listed first, with the child categories indented below:

Name
Toyota
— Prius
— Auris
— Land Cruiser
— Yaris

Here is a category widget for a site using the structure above:

Categories

Toyota
  Auris
  Land Cruiser
  Prius
  Yaris

You can see how it's possible to preserve the hierarchy in the widget.

Since we installed Yoast SEO as an essential plugin, we now have some extra control over our categories.

Click the **Edit** link underneath one of your categories. The first influence of Yoast SEO is the description editor:

You now have some formatting options. This is really useful when a theme includes the description at the top of a category page. The Twenty Twenty-One theme does this. Here is that Kenwood

Category page:

You can see the category description, with formatting and an image, is included at the top of the category page. All posts in the Kenwood category would be listed below.

But there is more. Scroll to the bottom of the edit category screen, and you'll see the Yoast SEO settings:

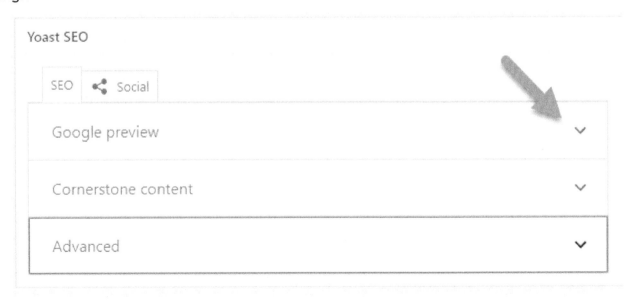

I've collapsed all the "tabs" to make the screenshot smaller. But each of those arrows on the right can open those sections.

The Google preview tab will show you what the category page will look like if listed on Google.

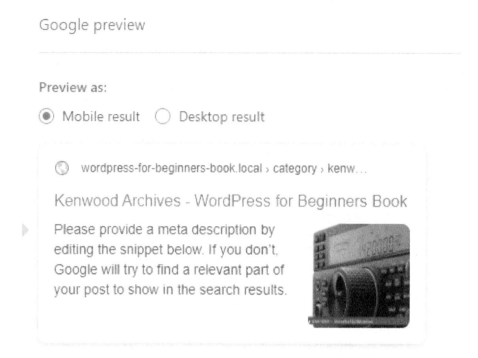

That screenshot shows the preview for **Mobile Results**, so check out what the category page listing would look like on a desktop computer. The radio selector is right above the preview.

That is your search engine listing, more or less. You can see that there is no meta description for that category page, but you can edit aspects of this listing underneath:

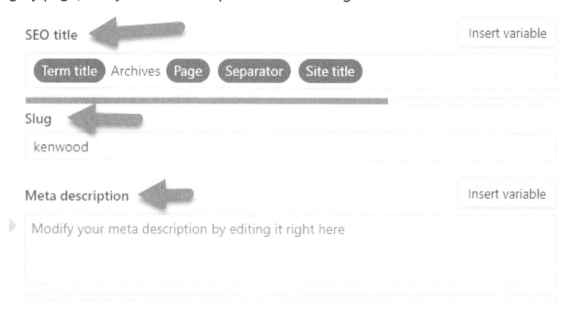

As you update these fields, you can watch how your listing appearance will change.

The **Advanced** "tab" will allow you to override the Yoast SEO plugin defaults for this category by choosing whether you want the category page to appear in the search results. Default is yes (that is how we set it up), but you can exclude the category page from the search results by overriding the default setting:

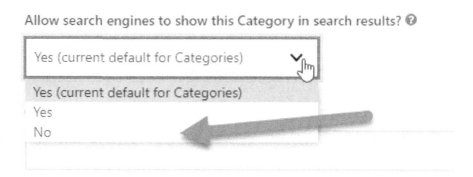

We won't be covering **Canonical URLs** in this book, but you can find out more if you want by clicking the little help button next to that entry.

The social tab allows you to specify title, description, and images that are used when your category page is shared on Facebook or Twitter.

Adding Tags

Adding Tags is very similar to adding categories, except tags cannot have a parent-child relationship with each other.

For every tag you enter, add a description to explain what that tag is being used for. That description will then be used for the Meta Description of the tag page; this is how we set it up within the SEO plugin, remember?

Like the categories, the **Add Tag** screen has just a few options – Title, Slug, and Description. You only need to fill in the Title and Description because WordPress will again handle the slug for us.

However, if you go in and edit an existing tag, you will see the same extra Yoast SEO settings we saw for categories. These are identical settings to the Category edit screen but do go in and have a look.

While I expect you will add tags directly on the **Add Post** screen as you write your content, I do highly recommend you come back to this section every time you use a new tag, just to fill in a description for those tags you create. Themes that support it will add that description to the top of the Tag page, which can be used creatively, so your tag page is not just a list of post titles.

When you make a new tag on the **Add Post** screen, you don't have the option of adding the description there and then, but it is important to add one nonetheless.

Tasks to Complete

1. Change the default **Uncategorized** category to something more useful.

2. Set up a few categories for your site.

3. Think about possible tags and keep a list on a notepad.

4. Make sure to add descriptions to every tag and category that you add.

Writing Posts

In this section of the book, I want to look at publishing content on your site. Version 5.0 of WordPress changed things dramatically. The old WYSIWYG editor (now called the Classic editor) was replaced by a page builder system called Gutenberg.

The two systems are VERY different.

The good news is that with the introduction of Gutenberg, WordPress created a "Classic Editor" plugin that can be installed, so you have a choice. You can use the new Gutenberg page builder or install the plugin and use the classic "WYSIWYG" editor. The choice is yours. If you want my opinion, I would recommend you go with the new Gutenberg editor as that is the future of WordPress and will introduce newer features that will extend your ability to build great looking posts and pages.

I will cover both editors in this chapter, so you know the main differences. Then, the choice is yours. However, the rest of the book will focus on Gutenberg only, since that is the editor built into WordPress.

If you want to install the Classic editor, install, and activate this plugin:

Once installed, click on the **Settings** link:

The plugin has added its settings to the **Writing** settings page, which makes sense considering this plugin helps you write content. There are two main settings you can change:

Default editor for all users	● Classic editor
	○ Block editor
Allow users to switch editors	○ Yes
	● No

The first one defines which editor you want to use by default. The Block editor option refers to Gutenberg. The second option is whether you want users to be able to switch back and forth between the Classic Editor and Gutenberg.

Choosing the Classic Editor or Gutenberg

If you want to use Gutenberg, then don't install the Classic Editor plugin. All posts and pages will then be created in the Gutenberg editor.

If you want to use the classic editor, install and activate the plugin. All "add post" and "add page" links will then default to the Classic editor.

Let's look at how you can add content, first using the Classic editor, then using Gutenberg. If you installed the Classic Editor plugin, then follow along. If you are intent on only using Gutenberg, then ignore this section.

The "Classic" WYSIWYG Editor

Click **Add New** in the **Posts** menu.

The Classic editor looks like this:

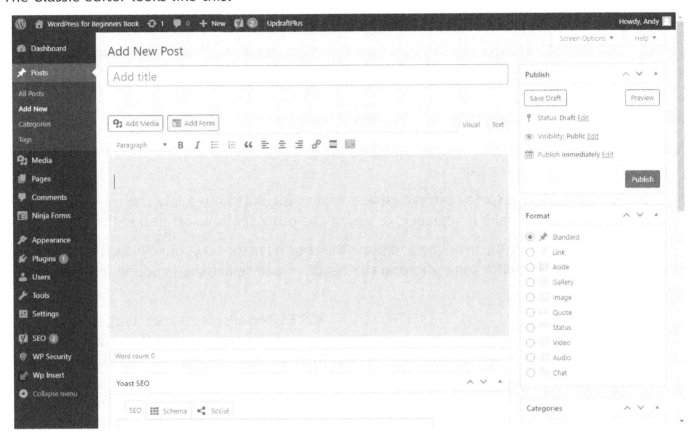

As I said, it is completely different from the default Gutenberg editor.

There is a box for the title and a large editor box for writing the content:

If you only see one line of buttons on your toolbar, click the **Toggle Toolbar** button on the far right. That will expand the toolbar.

You'll see on the top right there are two tabs, above and to the right of the toolbar – **Visual** & **Text**.

The Visual tab is where you can write your content using WYSIWYG features. On this tab, you'll see text and media formatted as it will appear on the website once published. This is the tab you will want to use for most of the work you do when adding new or editing existing content on your site.

The other tab – Text - shows the raw code that is responsible for the layout and content of the page. Unless you specifically need to insert some code or script into your content, stick with the Visual tab.

The two rows of buttons allow you to format your content visually. If you have used any type of Word Processor before, then this should be intuitive.

I won't go through the functions of all these buttons. If you need help understanding what a button does, move your mouse over it to get a popup help tooltip.

Adding content to your site is as easy as typing it into the large box under the toolbar. Just use it like you would any word processor.

Write your content. Select some text and click a formatting button to apply the format. Make it bold, or change its color, make it a header, or any of the other features offered in the toolbar.

To create a headline, enter the headline and press the return button on your keyboard to make sure it is on its own line. Now click somewhere in the headline and select the headline from the drop-down box in the toolbar.

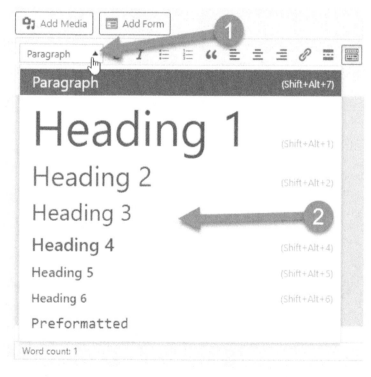

NOTE: WordPress themes typically show the title of your post as an H1 header at the top of the page. This is the biggest header available and is equivalent to the **Heading1** in the drop-down selector. You should not use more than one H1 header on a web page, so avoid using the **Heading 1** as you write your content. Use **Heading 2** for main sections within your article and **Heading 3** for sub-headers inside **Heading 2** sections.

OK, it's now time to go ahead and write the post for your website.

As you write your article, you may want to insert an image or some other form of media. We looked at the Media library earlier in the book, but let's go through the process of adding an image to an article.

Adding Images

The process is straightforward.

Position your cursor in the article where you want to add the image. Don't worry too much about getting it in the right place because you can always re-position it later if you need to.

Click the **Add Media** button located above the WYSIWYG editor, to the left, and you'll see the popup screen that we've seen previously:

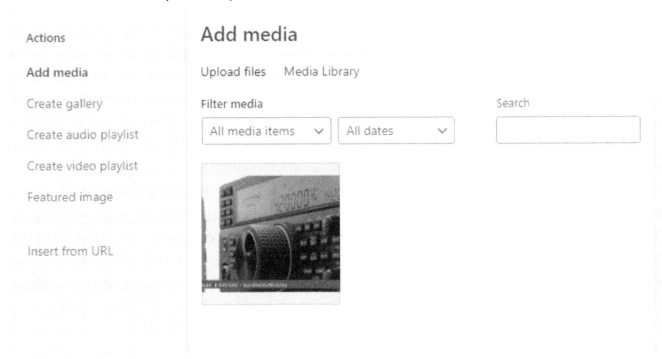

From this screen, you can select an image from the media library or click the **Upload Files** tab to upload a new image to the media library.

Let's add an image from our Media Library.

Click the **Media Library** tab if it is not already selected and click on the image you want to use in the post.

A checkmark appears in the top right corner of the image, and the "attachment" details are displayed on the right side. These image details can be edited if you want to.

At the bottom of the right sidebar is an **Insert into post** button. Before you click that, we should consider a few of the sidebar options.

One important option is the **Alt Text**. This text is read to the visually impaired visitors on your site and helps them understand what images are being shown. Therefore, add a short descriptive ALT text. For my example, **Kenwood Radio** is sufficient.

At the bottom of the right-hand column (you may need to scroll down) are some **Attachment Display Settings**. Currently, my image is set to "none" for alignment.

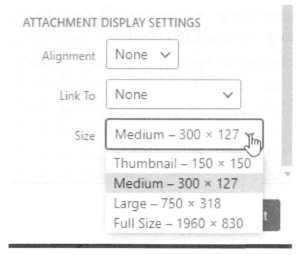

ATTACHMENT DISPLAY SETTINGS

Alignment: None

Link To: None

Size: Medium – 300 × 127

Thumbnail – 150 × 150
Medium – 300 × 127
Large – 750 × 318
Full Size – 1960 × 830

I want to align the image to the left so I can select that from the drop-down box. When an image is aligned left (or right) in WordPress, the post text wraps around it. If you select **None** or **Center** for alignment, the text won't wrap.

The next option you have is to link your image to something. The default setting is **None**, meaning we insert an image that is not clickable by the visitor because it is not linked to anything. Most of the time, I'll use none. However, if you want the image to open up when clicked (e.g., in a lightbox), then select **Media file**.

You can also link an image to an **Attachment page** (which we saw earlier) or a **Custom URL**.

The **Custom URL** option is really useful. This allows you to navigate to a URL when a user clicks an image. For example, if your image is a "Buy Now" button, you'd want the image linked to the purchase page.

The last of the display settings is **Size**. You'll be able to choose from a range of available options.

The dimensions are included with each file size, so choose the one that is closest to the size you want the image to appear on your page.

Once you have made your selection, click the **Insert into post** button at the button.

Here is that image inserted into my post at the position of my cursor:

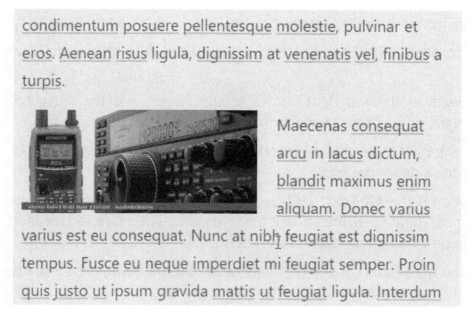

condimentum posuere pellentesque molestie, pulvinar et eros. Aenean risus ligula, dignissim at venenatis vel, finibus a turpis.

Maecenas consequat arcu in lacus dictum, blandit maximus enim aliquam. Donec varius varius est eu consequat. Nunc at nibh feugiat est dignissim tempus. Fusce eu neque imperdiet mi feugiat semper. Proin quis justo ut ipsum gravida mattis ut feugiat ligula. Interdum

If you have the position wrong, you can simply click the image to select it and drag the image to a different location.

If you find that the image isn't inserted as you intended (e.g., you forgot to align it), click on the image. A toolbar appears above the image and a bounding box around it:

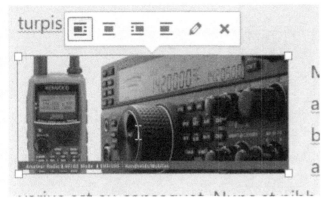

The bounding box includes a small square in each corner. You can use this to resize the image. Drag one of the corners to make the image bigger or smaller.

The first four buttons in the toolbar allow you to re-align the image.

The last button in the toolbar will delete the image.

The toolbar edit button looks like a pencil. You can use this to open the **Image Details** screen to make a number of changes:

You'll also see a link to **Advanced Options** at the bottom. Click that to expand the advanced options:

One of the most useful advanced options is the **Open link in a new tab** option. When someone clicks the image, whatever it is linked to opens in a new browser tab.

Once you have made your edits on this screen, click the **Update** button, and the changes will be updated in your post.

You can insert videos from your Media library in the same way.

OK, finish your first post.

Something to try: We added an image that was already in the Media Library. Go ahead and add an image from your hard disk. After clicking the Add Media button, you'll need to go to the Upload tab to proceed. Try it and see if you can successfully add an image this way.

Once you've done that, try adding an image to a post by dragging and dropping the image from your computer directly into the WYSIWYG editor window.

It's all very intuitive.

There are a few things we need to do before we publish a post, so let's go through the complete sequence from the start to publish:

1. Add a post title.

2. Write & format your post using the visual text editor (WYSIWYG).

3. Select a post format if available. You can ignore this option for most posts you add.

4. Select a category.

5. Add some tags if you want to. Tags can always be added later, so don't feel under any pressure to add them now. Of course, you can also decide you don't want to use tags on your site. That is fine too.

6. Add an excerpt.

7. Select a date/time if you want to schedule the post for the future.

8. Publish/Schedule the post.

OK, so far, we have completed down to step 2.

Post Formats

One of the sections in the Classic editor is the post formats. Here they are for my Twenty Twenty-One theme:

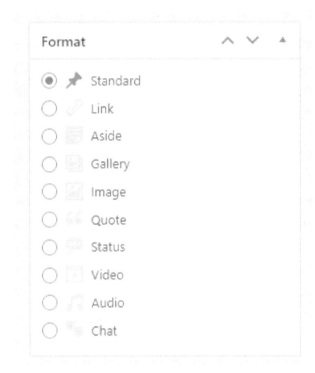

Post formats are different layouts built into the theme. When you have entered a post, play around with the post format, and see what effect each format has on the layout and style.

Most people never get around to using post formats, but it is nice to know they are there if you need them.

If you are interested in post formats, you can read more about them on the WordPress websites:

https://wordpress.org/support/article/post-formats/

Post Category

The next step in our publishing sequence is to choose a category. Choose just one category for each post.

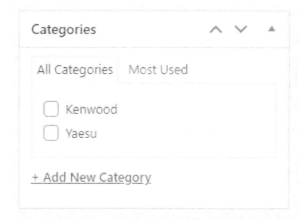

If you forget to check a category box, WordPress will automatically use your default category.

You can add a new category "on the fly" from within the **Add post** screen, but if you do, remember to go in and write a description for the new category so it can be used as the meta description of that category page (remember the Yoast SEO plugin we set up earlier is expecting a description of categories and tags).

Post Tags

If you want to use tags for the post, you can type them directly into the tags box, even if they don't already exist. Just type them in, separated by commas. When you are finished typing the tags, click the **Add** button to the right of the tags box.

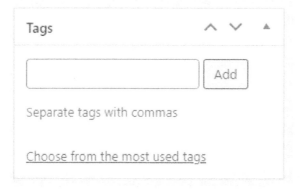

As you add and use more tags, you can click on **Choose from the most used tags,** and a box will appear with some of the tags you've used before. You can just click the tags that apply, and they'll be added to the tag list of your post.

If you add new tags when entering a post, remember to go into the Tags settings to write a short description for each one. Yes, it takes time, but it is worth that description on the tag page.

Post Excerpt

You should add a post excerpt to all posts. If you don't see an excerpt entry box on your screen, check the **Screen Options** to make sure **Excerpt** is checked.

NOTE: Screen options are not available if you are using the Gutenberg editor, but that doesn't matter as excerpts are enabled by default in Gutenberg.

Screen elements

Some screen elements can be shown or hidden by using the checkboxes. They can be expanded and collapsed by clickling on their and arranged by dragging their headings or by clicking on the up and down arrows.

☑ Format   ☑ Categories   ☑ Tags   ☑ Append a Ninja Form   ☑ Featured image   ☑ Yoast SEO   ☑ Excerpt   ☐ Send T

☐ Custom Fields   ☐ Discussion   ☐ Slug   ☐ Author

Layout

◯ 1 column   ◉ 2 columns

Additional settings

Once checked, the **Excerpt** box magically appears at the bottom of your edit post screen.

Excerpt   ∧   ∨   ▲

Excerpts are optional hand-crafted summaries of your content that can be used in your theme. Learn more about manual excerpts.

The excerpt should be a short description of the post you are writing. Its purpose is to encourage visitors to click through and read the article (e.g., From the search engine). This excerpt will be used as the Meta description tag of the post, as well as the description of the post in the "related posts" section, which is displayed at the end of each article you publish (see the YARPP plugin later).

Enter a three to five-sentence excerpt that encourages the click.

Publishing the Post

The next step in the process is deciding when you want the post to go live on your site. Let's look at the **Publish** section of the screen.

The first option you have is to save the post as a draft.

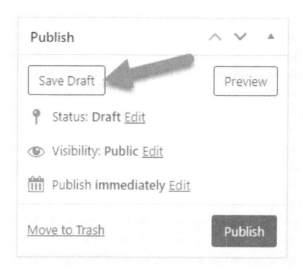

Once saved as a draft, you can go back at any time to make changes or publish the article. Draft posts are not shown on your site. To be visible on your website, you need to publish the post.

If you want it up there immediately, then click the Publish button. If, like me, you are writing several posts in a batch, it is a good idea to spread the posting of the content out a little bit. Luckily, WordPress allows us to schedule posts in the future.

The default is to publish **immediately**. However, there is an **Edit** link you can click to open a scheduling calendar:

Enter the date and time you want to publish the post and then click the OK button.

The publish button now changes to **Schedule**.

Click the **Schedule** button to schedule the post.

That's it. You've just published or scheduled your first WordPress post using the Classic editor.

If you now click on the **All Posts** in the sidebar menu, you will see your new post listed. If you selected the option to allow users to switch editor (when we set up the Classic editor plugin), you are given the option of editing the post in the Classic Editor (which created the post) or the Block Editor (Gutenberg).

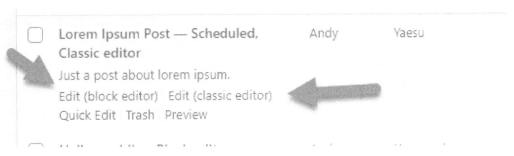

If you did not select the option to allow switching of the editor, you'd just have a single standard edit link. If you need to change that setting, go to the Settings, Writing screen to make the change, and don't forget to save those changes.

The Gutenberg Editor

NOTE: This section will take you through the basics of using the Gutenberg editor. Written text and screenshots are all very well, but I feel that video would be a better medium for teaching you how to use this editor. I, therefore, created a Gutenberg course that **readers of my book can get for free** (at least during 2022). You can find a link to it on the updates page for this book:

https://ezseonews.com/wp2022/

Gutenberg is the default editor in WordPress, so I will be focusing on it from now on. In fact, I am going to deactivate and delete the Classic Editor plugin before I type another word.

OK, that's done. My table of posts in the All Post screen now only shows the Edit/Quick Edit links:

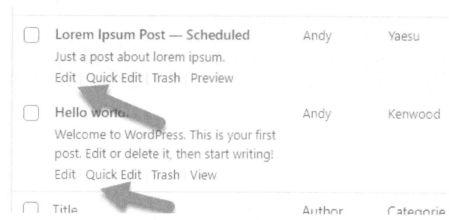

But these links open up the Gutenberg editor now the Classic plugin has been removed.

If you want to stick with Gutenberg, I recommend you remove the Classic Editor plugin.

If you've ever used a WordPress "page builder" like Elementor, then Gutenberg will seem a lot more familiar to you. Like other page builders, Gutenberg uses a system of blocks to help you build your content.

When you now open a post or page that was created with the Classic editor, any content you created in the Classic editor will be contained in a single **Classic Block**. Click to select the block and you'll see an option to **Convert to blocks**.

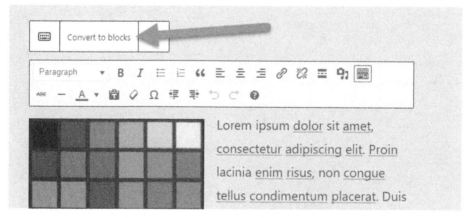

Since we are now working exclusively with Gutenberg, click that button.

You'll find that the content will now be divided up into discrete Gutenberg blocks. Each block can now be selected and manipulated in isolation from the rest of the content. Make sure you **Update** your post to save this change.

OK, click on the **Add New** post link in the sidebar menu. If you find the sidebar menu is missing, you are in **Full Screen** mode. Click on the **Options** button and deselect the **Fullscreen mode**.

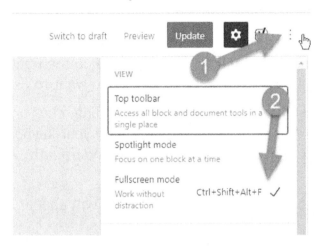

When you add a new post or page, you'll be greeted with the Gutenberg editor:

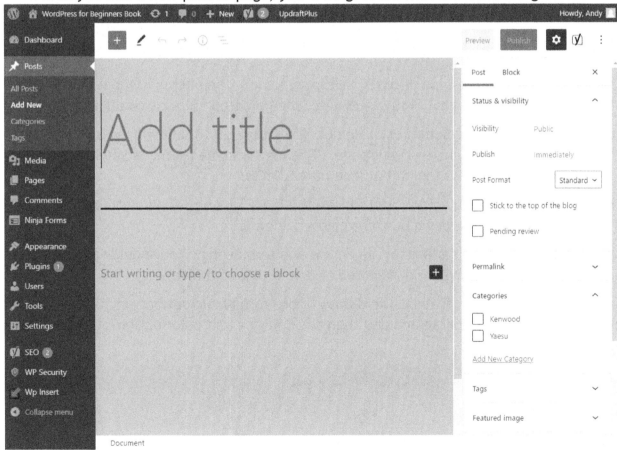

There is a simple prompt: **Add title**.

Click into that box, and you can type the title of your post.

Under the title you'll see this:

Type / to choose a block   [+]

If you want to just add text, you can just click where it says **Type/to choose a block** and start typing. By default, this is a paragraph block. The + button on the right allows you to switch the block from a paragraph block to any other type of block you want to use.

However, if you just want to add some text below the heading, click on the block and start typing. Try it. Type a sentence of text and press the ENTER key on your keyboard. The editor will save that text as a paragraph block, and create a new prompt underneath, which is the same prompt you saw above.

If you select the paragraph block you just created, a menu will appear above the block:

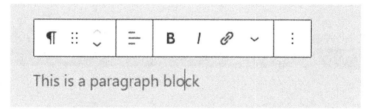

This is a paragraph block

The first button indicates the type of block that is selected. The pilcrow symbol indicates a paragraph block. If you click that, you can convert the paragraph block to a different type.

The second button with two columns of three dots is a **Drag** button, allowing you to drag the block up or down in the block sequence on your page. This may become useful as you add more blocks to your page, but I have always found it a little hit and miss.

The third button(s) are **Up/Down** options to move the block one position up or down. Click the up button to move it up, and the down button to move it down.

The other buttons in this toolbar are for alignment and formatting. You should recognize the link button, which allows you to hyperlink selected text to a URL of choice.

The drop-down arrow on the far right offers a few more formatting options, including text color. Select a sentence from your paragraph and then click on this text color option. Choose a color and see what happens:

Quisque et elit facilisis ex eleifend convallis. Integer tempus, diam eleifend varius rhoncus, nibh tortor dignissim nisi, a lobortis eros sem sed enim. Pellentesque habitaddfnt morbi tristique senectus et netus et malesuada fames ac turpis egestas. Mauris tincidunt interdum accumsan.

The other options in that menu work the same way.

The final button in the toolbar is the **More Options** button. This menu offers easy ways to add a new block before or after the current one and a few other useful features (including removing the block) and grouping blocks.

OK, let's add an image after the above paragraph block. When you pressed the **Enter** key after creating your first paragraph block, a new one was created underneath. It because of the + button on the right.

There are a few ways to add a specific type of block. The one I like the most is the / key on your keyboard. Make sure your editing cursor is in the new block you just created and type a forward slash (/). A popup menu appears with the most common blocks:

I can select **Image** from that list, and the block will become an image block.

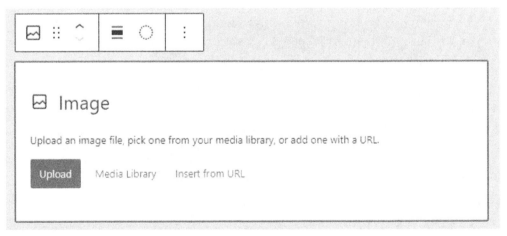

Notice that the toolbar menu on this block is a little different. This menu will change because it will only offer features that are compatible with the image block.

To insert an image, I can click **Upload** to choose one from my computer. During that upload, the image will be added automatically to the media library.

Another option is to click **Media Library** to open the library and add an image in the usual way.

The final option in that menu is to insert the image from a URL. This would mean the image is already on a web page somewhere. I should just remind you that images have copyright protection, so make sure you have permission to use images on other websites.

There is another option to insert an image that I use. From my computer, I can drag and drop an image directly onto the image block.

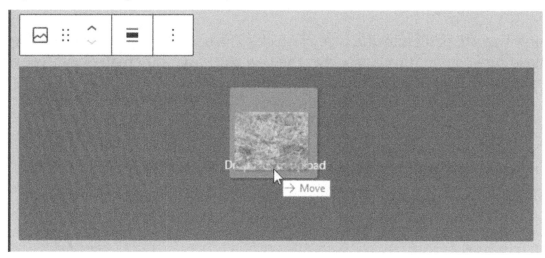

When you drop the image onto the block, it is uploaded to the media library and to the image block.

The menu on top of the image gives you a lot of options. Play with them to see what you can do.

Using the Forward Slash to Add Blocks

When you added a block and type a forward slash (/), the popup showed common blocks. But what if the block you want to use is not in that popup? For example, what if I want to insert a video? If you check back, the video block was not in that popup.

Well, the solution is to type the / followed by the name of the block you want to use. e.g., if I type /v into the empty block, here is the popup:

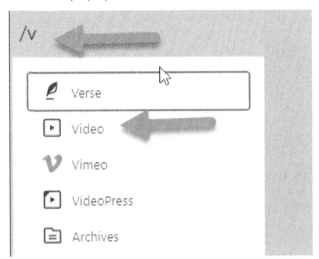

Video is now on that list, and I can select it.

When you first start out with Gutenberg, you won't know what blocks are available. Therefore, I suggest you start off by clicking the + button in the top toolbar:

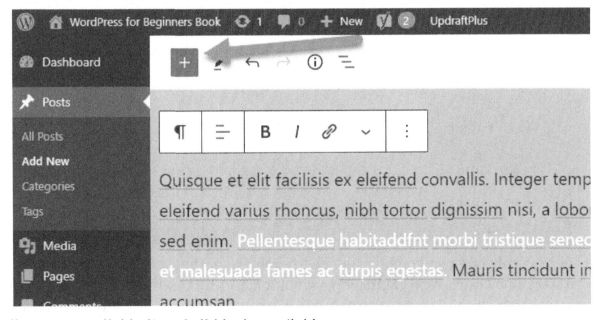

That will open a scrollable list of all blocks available:

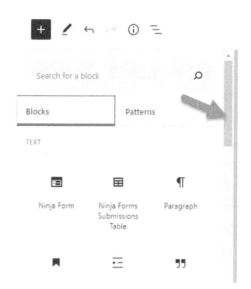

Go on. Open it and scroll down the list to see the range of blocks that are available to you. With Gutenberg, you build your web pages using these blocks.

In its simplest form, a post could be simply a title and a **paragraph** block, like this:

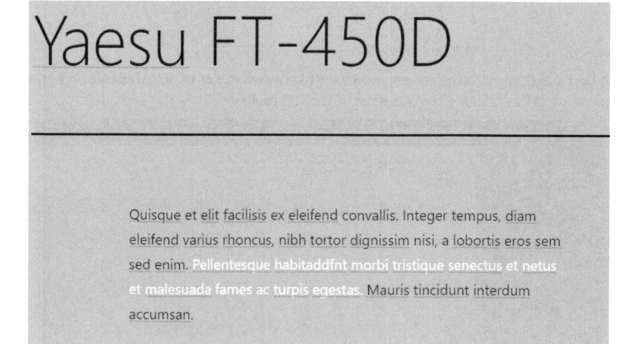

Yaesu FT-450D

Quisque et elit facilisis ex eleifend convallis. Integer tempus, diam eleifend varius rhoncus, nibh tortor dignissim nisi, a lobortis eros sem sed enim. Pellentesque habitaddfnt morbi tristique senectus et netus et malesuada fames ac turpis egestas. Mauris tincidunt interdum accumsan.

Note that there is only one paragraph per block. If you are writing a block of text and press the Enter key to start a new paragraph, Gutenberg will automatically create a new paragraph block for the second paragraph. In the following screenshot, I pressed the Enter key after the final word of the first paragraph:

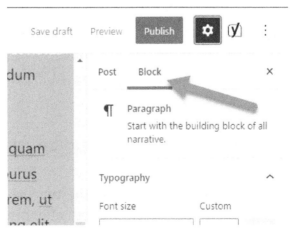

Can you see that Gutenberg automatically created a new paragraph block? Go on and try it for yourself.

This auto-addition of new paragraph blocks makes writing long pieces of content very easy because you do not need to create paragraph blocks as you type manually.

If you tend to write your content in an external editor and then paste it into WordPress, you'll find that Gutenberg automatically splits the text into multiple paragraph blocks for you!

The advantage of using one block per paragraph is that each paragraph can then be formatted independently of the others.

Paragraph Block Properties

All blocks have their own properties. Since we've added a paragraph block, let's check out the properties because you can do some interesting stuff. Click into a paragraph block. On the right-hand side, you should see the **Block** tab has been selected:

If you don't see the properties block at all, click on the small **Cog** button. You can see it in that screenshot above, right next to the **Publish** button.

The **Block** tab shows you the settings for that block only (as opposed to the **Post** tab, which has settings affecting the entire post).

At the top of the paragraph block properties, you can select the size of the text for that paragraph:

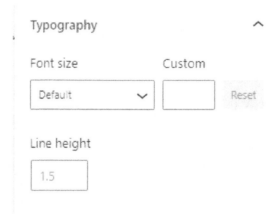

Either select a size from the **Font Size** drop-down box (try it!) or by typing in a custom size.

You can also define how much space is between each row of text in the line height box.

The next set of options for this block are the **Color Settings**. You can change both the text color and background color. Try these out.

The next paragraph option is for a drop cap. The **Drop Cap** option can add some interest to your paragraph:

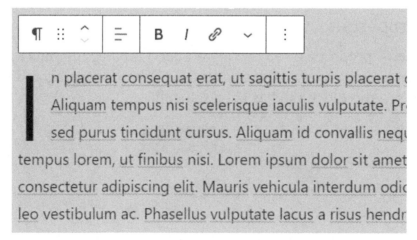

The options in this panel are in addition to the ones in the toolbar right above the currently selected block.

The formatting options available will obviously depend on the type of block you have selected, but the theme can also play a part. Some features like full-width alignment may be available for some blocks, but only if the theme supports it.

Before we leave this block, I wanted to mention the **More Options** button and go through a few of its options.

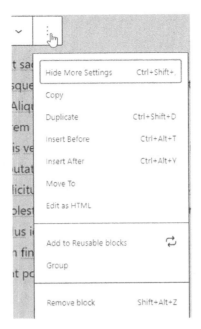

From this menu, you can duplicate the block, insert a block before or after the current one, and edit the block as HTML.   The final option allows you to delete the block.

But there are two features I want to look at in more detail.

Reusable Blocks

This is an interesting feature. It means you can create a block and save it so that it can be reused across your site, on different posts and pages. If you update the reusable block, you update it everywhere you use it.

As an example, lets create a copyright notice and save as a reusable block:

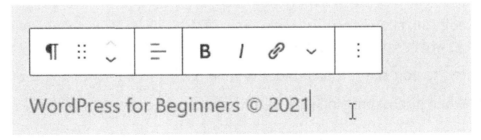

Clicking the **Options** button, I can now **Add to Reusable Blocks.** You'll be asked to name your block, so I'll call mine, Copyright.

Now click on the + button in the toolbar at the top and click onto the **Reusable** tab. You'll see your new reusable block.

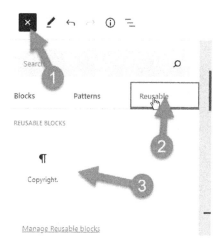

This will appear on this tab whenever you are creating a post or page, so you can insert it.

When the date changes over to the next year, click the **Manage Reusable Blocks** link that you see at the bottom of the block viewer to be taken to a table showing all reusable blocks you've created.

You can click the edit link and change the year from 2021 to 2022. This change will be updated on every post and page where you've used this block.

What if I just wanted to edit the reusable block on one page without affecting it on other pages?

You can do that. When a reusable block is inserted into a post or page, select it to show the popup menu:

Click that first button to **Show Reusable Block.**

The menu changes:

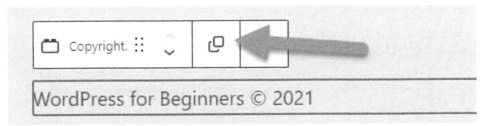

Now click on the **Convert to Regular Blocks** button.

Your reusable block on this page will be converted to a regular block that you can now edit without affecting the reusable block you saved, or that reusable block on any other page of the site.

The other menu item I want to look at briefly (again) is the Group option. This creates a group containing your chosen blocks. You can then add more blocks to that group. Once you've created your group, you can save it as a re-useable block if you want.

Add a heading block and type "Sign up for my newsletter".

Now add a paragraph underneath and type some text about how you "won't share details with other companies".

Now add a button block underneath and change the label of the button to "Subscribe".

Here is mine:

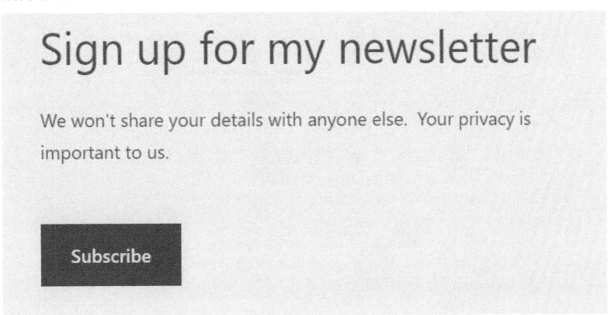

Select the headline, then SHIFT + mouse click the other two blocks in turn to select all three. From the options menu, select **Group**. All three blocks are now added to the group, which you can select:

If you have trouble selecting the group, don't forget you can do it via the **List View** menu at the top.

Now from the **Options** menu, select **Add to reusable blocks**. Add a title.

Update your post and add a new post.

Click the + in the toolbar at the top, and select the **Reusable** tab. Add the Subscription block you just saved.

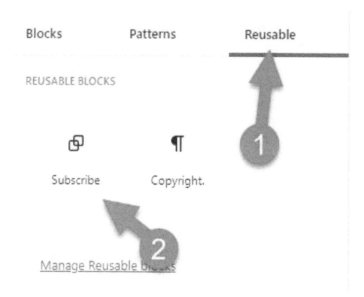

See how easy that was?

One of the benefits of using groups is that the group then has its own properties in the right panel:

All the blocks in the group can be manipulated as a single group. For example, by changing the background and font colors of the group:

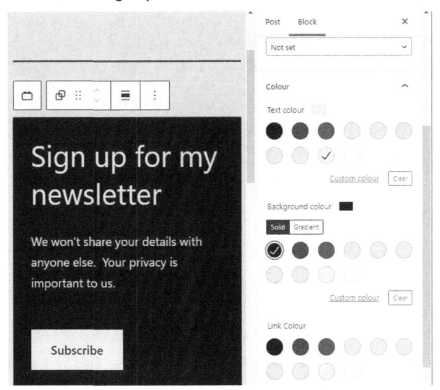

Moving a Block in Gutenberg

Click inside the block you want to move.

Now, look at the buttons in the toolbar.

One of them has six dots arranged in two columns of three. This button allows you to drag and drop the block to the desired location:

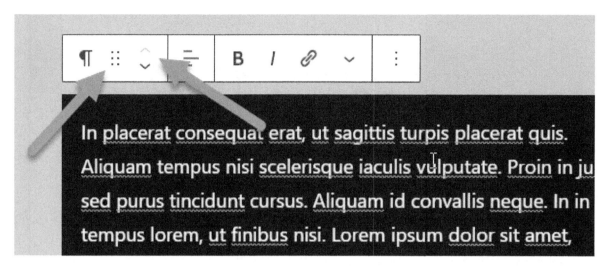

Just click and hold the mouse button down on this block, and the cursor will change to a little hand. If you start to drag the block, it disappears, and you get a horizontal line that represents its position. Drag the line up or down to the desired location and drop:

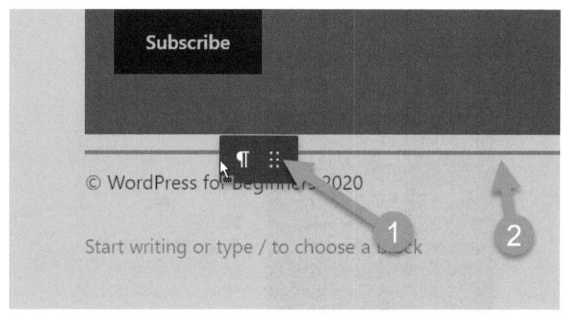

I find the drag and drop option is still quite fiddly, so I prefer the second option.

In the toolbar above the block, you want to move are two arrows. One will move the block up one position, and the other will move the block down one position. This is my preferred method of moving blocks.

Inserting Blocks in Between Existing Blocks

Each block in your post will display the toolbar at the top when you click on it. The right-hand button is the **More Options** menu that gives you the opportunity to insert a block before or after the current one.

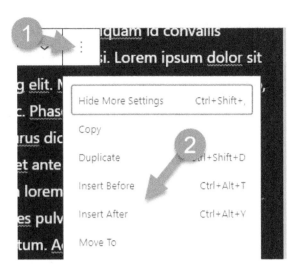

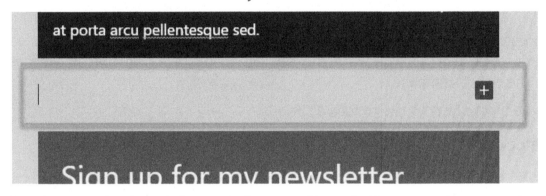

These options will insert a blank block which you can then work with:

Also, note that there are keyboard shortcuts for some items in the menu. For example, if you want to insert a block before an existing block, click the block and use the keyboard shortcut Ctrl+Alt+T (or the Mac equivalent). Ctrl + Alt + Y will insert after the current block.

Delete a Block

We have already seen this, but let's recap.

1. Select the block you want to remove.
2. From the menu at the top, click the button with three vertical dots.
3. Select **Remove Block**, or press SHIFT+ALT+Z on your keyboard.

So, we have the basics of adding, deleting, and moving blocks. What blocks are actually available?

Available "Building" Blocks

The blocks manager (accessed by the + in the top left) divides blocks into groups, including text blocks, media blocks, design blocks, widgets, and embeds.

Here are a few that you will probably find yourself using regularly.

- Paragraph
- Image
- Heading
- List
- Quote
- Video
- Table
- Buttons
- Columns
- Spacer

I won't go through all of the blocks that are available, as I want you to explore. It's easy. Create a post and add some blocks. Play with the settings in the block toolbar as well as the block properties in the right-hand pane.

There are three blocks I would like to look at briefly.

The Table Block

Creating a table used to be a chore when the Classic editor was the default WordPress editor. It meant having to create the table in HTML and insert it manually into the code of the post or page.

The table block in Gutenberg makes it very easy. You'll find it in the Text blocks section or by creating a new block and typing /t

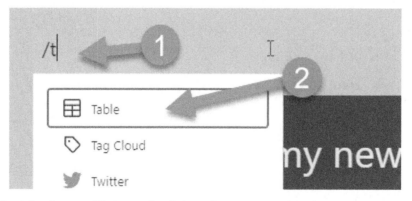

When you add a table block, you'll be asked for the row and column count. You can always edit this later by adding new columns or rows, but it is easier if you know now and can enter the precise dimensions.

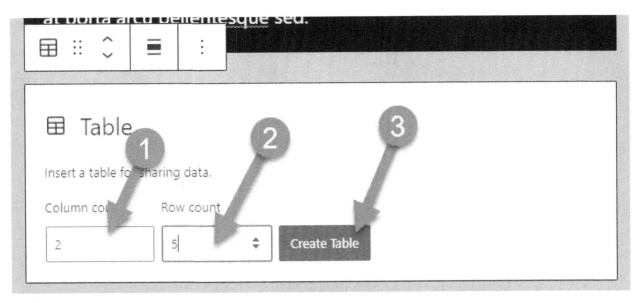

On clicking **Create Table**, you'll have a nicely formatted table awaiting data.

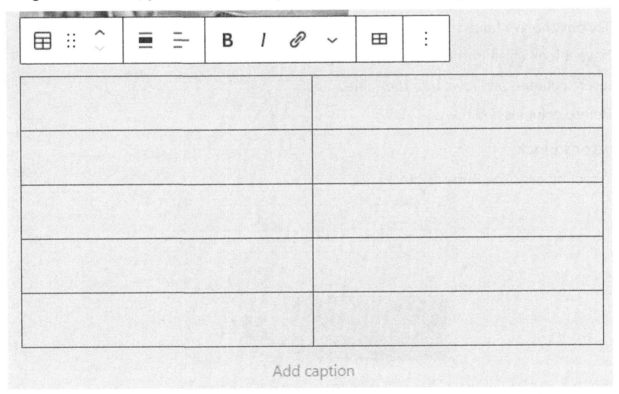

Add caption

Notice the toolbar at the top. The **Edit Table** button gives you the power to add or delete cells:

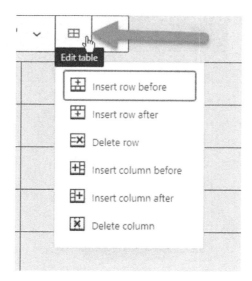

You can explore the table block for yourself. Try this:

1. Create a table and try adding data to it.

2. Try out the available styles in the block properties.

3. Have a look at all of the table block properties.

4. Insert columns and rows into the table.

5. Delete columns and rows.

The Buttons Block

Another cool block is the **Buttons** block.

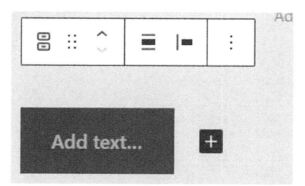

When you add the button block, the caption of the button says **Add text...**, so type something in:

The buttons block allows you to create several buttons in a row. When you have finished typing the caption of the first button, press the Return (Enter) key on your keyboard. Another button will be created:

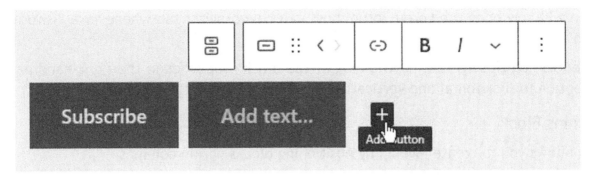

If you do this by accident, select the button you want to remove and use the **Options** button to remove the button.

When a button is selected, you can use the **Link** button in the toolbar to specify a URL to visit when that button is clicked. Maybe the button is a buy button, and you need to link it to a PayPal URL?

Alternatively, you might want to link the button to an existing page on your site. Let's see how to do that.

Select the button and click on the **Link** button in the block's toolbar. Start typing in some text from the title of the post you want to link to, and it should pop up for you to select:

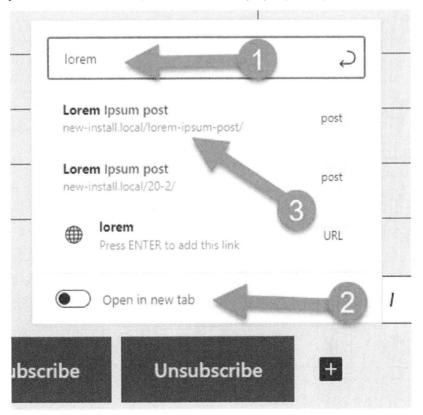

You can see the Lorem Ipsum world post was found. If I want the button to open the post in a new browser tab, select that option first, then select the post.

The button will now open the Lorem Ipsum post in a new browser tab whenever a visitor clicks on the button

With the button block selected, have a look at the block properties in the right-hand pane. You have the option for horizontal and vertical arrangement of the buttons in the block.

The Columns Block

This block allows you to create layouts by positioning blocks within columns.

Add a columns block, and you'll see this:

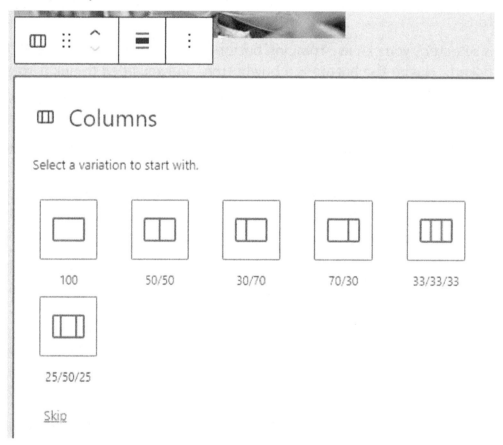

Choose the option that is closest to what you want to achieve. I'll choose the three-column layout 33/33/33:

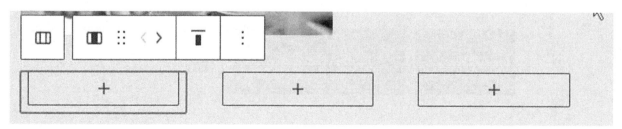

I can now add blocks to each of the three columns by clicking on the + symbol in the middle of the column. What makes columns so powerful is that you can add more than one block to each column. In the following screenshot, I have added an image to the first column.

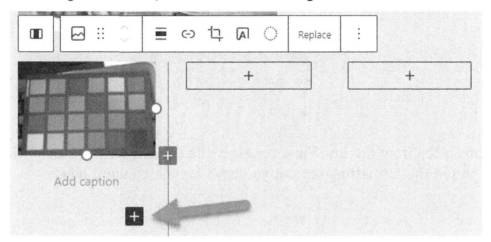

When I select that image, you can see the option to add another block underneath.

Select the columns block from the **List View** button at the top:

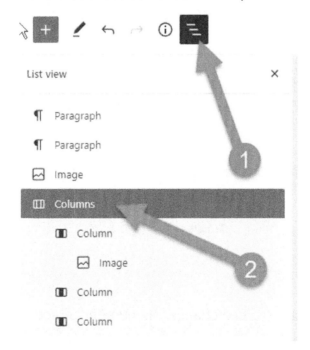

You can see the **Columns** block and any blocks contained inside.

Add a paragraph block (with some text) under the image in the first column, then come back and look at the **List View** again. You'll see the paragraph has been added under the image, both nestled inside the first column.

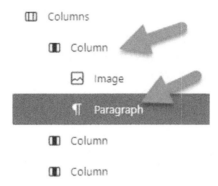

Select the **Columns** block from the **List View** to select the entire columns block. Now look at the properties panel to see the formatting options you have for the columns block:

There are a couple of styles, but you can change the number of columns:

If an individual column is selected (use the **List View** button to select the second column), you get the properties for that specific column. can change its width.

Have a play around with those settings. You won't break anything.

What happens if you select a block inside one of the columns?

Columns are quite cool!

Yoast SEO Settings for the Post

When we installed the Yoast SEO plugin, it added a panel to the add post (and add page) screen. We saw this earlier when dealing with categories. You will find this Yoast SEO box of tricks wherever you are setting up or defining something that will become a web page on your site. That means when you are adding/editing categories, tags, posts, and pages.

If you scroll down a little, you should come across the **Yoast SEO** section.

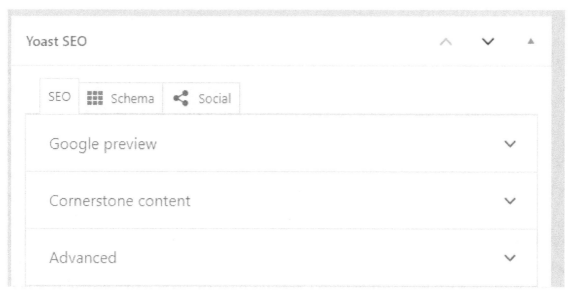

This Yoast SEO box looks like the ones we saw earlier. In this case, there are three tabs across the top. SEO, Schema, and Social.

The SEO Tab

At the top, we have the **Google Preview** section. We saw this when we looked at adding categories. Go back and refer to that section of the book as the same principles apply, just this time to posts.

The Cornerstone content section is something I don't personally use in this plugin. If you want to learn more, click to open that section, and visit the link:

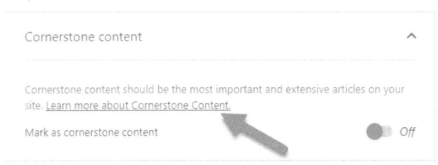

Some of the more powerful features of this plugin can be found in the **Advanced** section of the SEO tab. We covered it briefly when we looked at categories, but let's go over it again in a little more detail.

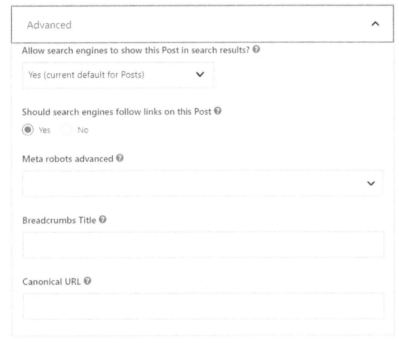

These settings give us fine control over how the search engines will deal with this post. We can use these settings to override the global settings for the site. This is powerful. With this fine level of control, we can treat every post and page on our site differently if we want to.

The top setting allows us to show/hide a post from the search engines. By default, all posts will be indexed by the search engines. If we don't want a post indexed and visible in the search engines, we can select **No** from the drop-down box (which sets the page to noindex and excludes it from the sitemap). However, this would be most unusual for posts.

The next setting is whether search engines should follow links in this post. The default is yes, but we can set them to no (which is a nofollow tag for those that know what this means). I don't recommend changing this unless you know what you are doing.

The **Meta Robots Advanced** allows us to set a few other Meta tags on our pages. Click on the field, and a drop-down box appears with selectable options:

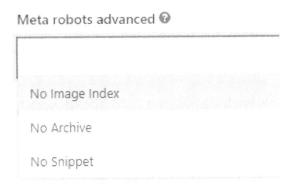

No Image Index is useful if you don't want the search engines to index the images on your page. Indexed images can be easily found within the image search on Google and pirated.

No Archive tag tells Google not to store a cached copy of your page. There are times when we don't want Google to keep an archive (cached version) of a page. By setting the post as **No Archive,** we are preventing the search engines from keeping a backup of the page.

Why might you want to do this?

Well, maybe you have a limited offer on your site, and you don't want people seeing it after the offer has finished. If the page was archived, it is technically possible for someone to go in and see the last cached page at Google, which will still show your previous offer.

No Snippet tells Google not to show a description under your Google listing (nor will it show a cached link in the search results).

The Schema Tab

Schema is a way of giving search engines more information about your content. In return, search engines like Google can create "rich" snippets in the search results that help your content stand out from the crowd:

www.bbcgoodfood.com › Recipes

Best ever chocolate brownies recipe - BBC Good Food

Ingredients. 185g unsalted butter. 185g best dark **chocolate**. 85g plain flour. 40g **cocoa** powder. 50g white **chocolate**. 50g milk **chocolate**. 3 large eggs. 275g golden caster sugar

★★★★★ Rating: 5 · 1,990 reviews · 1 hr · Calories: 150

The short version is that different types of web content are marked up with different schema designed to provide information about that type of content.

The long version is that it is complicated and beyond the scope of this book.

While it is nice to know that Yoast SEO tries to help with schema, this plugin would only be scratching the surface in the way it helps implement schema.

The Social Tab

We saw this earlier in the book with categories. It allows you to specify an image, title, and description for Facebook and Twitter whenever anyone tries to share your webpage.

OK, that's it for the Yoast SEO box. Before we go any further, I want to disable a couple of features of the Yoast SEO plugin. These are SEO analysis and Readability. It's up to you if you want to keep them enabled. Some people like the idea of a plugin that can give SEO recommendations, but, the plugin is just counting keywords so that you can optimize your page around a single keyword. That used to work a few years back but optimizing a page for a single keyword today will get your page kicked out of Google. The readability score is just a feature I don't use.

To deactivate these, click on **SEO** in the sidebar menu of the dashboard.

On the **General** page, click on the **Features** tab.

You can now switch these features off:

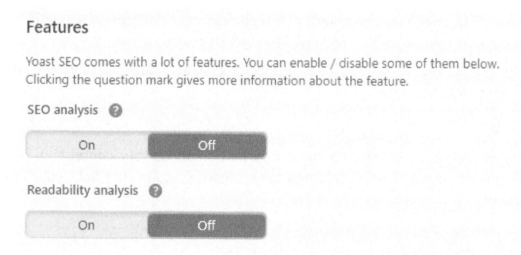

If you decide to keep these enabled, be aware that you'll have the extra information relating to these features in your dashboard. They won't be in my screenshots from now on.

Post (Document) Properties

As you work on your post or page, you have access to the **Post** properties on the right:

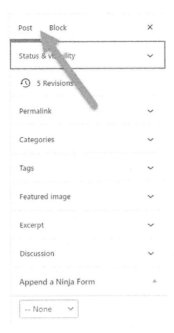

I have closed all of the sections so I can fit them all in a single screenshot.

These settings allow you to set the category of a post, add tags, set a featured image, create an excerpt, etc. We typically use these settings as we prepare a post for publishing.

Let's go through the process.

The Process for Publishing a Post

Once you have written your post, there are a few other things you may want to do before hitting the publish button. Let's look at the typical workflow:

1. Write a post.

2. Choose a category.

3. Add tags.

4. Insert featured image.

5. Add an excerpt.

6. Check/edit permalink (slug) of the post.

7. Publish or schedule.

I'll assume you have created your post and you want to go through and publish it. Let's go through the steps:

1. Choose category

From the Post properties, open the **Categories** section:

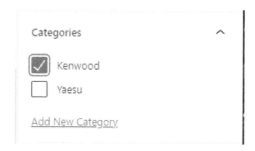

Select the desired category from the list, or **Add a New Category** if you want, directly from the Gutenberg editor.

2. Add tags

In the **Tags** section, add a list of comma-separated words and phrases you want to use as tags. When you type a comma, the editor will add whatever came before the comma as a tag.

3. Insert featured image

Featured images can be used by your theme, e.g., as an image next to each post on an archive page (e.g. Category or tag). Just click the **Set Featured Image** button to add an image from the media library (or upload).

4. Add an excerpt

Open the excerpt section and type in a paragraph about your post. This can be used by themes and/or plugins as a post summary, e.g., on recent post lists.

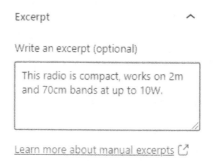

5. Check/edit permalink (slug) of the post.

You will remember that we set up the permalink structure when we set up WordPress. WordPress will handle the creation of permalinks (post URLs) for us, so there is no need to do anything. However, we do have an option to manually edit the permalinks on a post by post basis. For an unpublished post, if you look at the permalinks section of Gutenberg, a temporary permalink is assigned:

When you publish the post, the permalink will be updated to use the structure we previously defined when setting up the **Permalinks** for the site.

This is what I chose:

On publishing, I am expecting the permalink to change to include the post category and post name. We'll come back and check after the final part of the publishing process.

6. Publish or schedule

At this point in the process, you can save the post as a draft. This will mean it is not published or live on the site but will be saved as it is. This is useful if you are working on a document but don't finish it in one sitting. Save it as a draft, and then come back later to finish and publish. The **Save draft** link is up there near the **Publish** button:

The Publish (or Update) button at the top can be used to publish your post or schedule it for future automatic publishing. Click it once, and you'll be asked to confirm you want to publish. Confirm by clicking the Publish again, and the post will go live. So, let's check that permalink section again:

Permalink

URL Slug

lorem-ipsum-post

The last part of the URL. Read about permalinks

View Post

http://new-install.local/uncategorized/lorem-ipsum-post/

As expected, the permalink now includes category (uncategorized) and post name (taken from the post title). There is also a new editable field called URL slug. I can now change the slug if I want for this post by directly editing that field.

Why might you do that?

Well, your post title may be quite long.

E.g., let's say "10 reasons to not upgrade to windows 10 just yet." The slug that would be generated would be **10-reasons-to-not-upgrade-to-windows-10-just-yet.**

Long, isn't it?

That means the URL for the post will be really long. In cases like this, I might edit the slug to something more manageable like **dont-upgrade-windows-10-yet**. Still quite long, but better.

So that's the routine for publishing a post. Let's have a look at the publishing options in a little more detail because you can also schedule posts, so they are automatically published at some date and time in the future.

Publishing & Scheduling Posts in Gutenberg

The top item in the post properties is **Status & Visibility**. These options allow us to publish and schedule content, as well as to choose the post format (we saw post formats earlier) and even send the post to trash.

At the top, you'll see that the **Visibility** is set to **Public** by default. This means that once published, the post will be visible to anyone that comes to your site. If you click the **Public** link, you'll see that you can also set posts to **Private** or **Password Protected**.

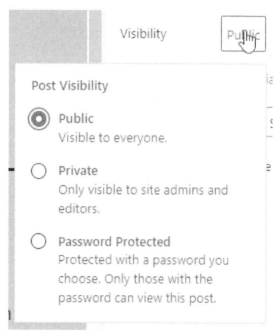

These are self-explanatory so read the brief description of each.

Under the **Visibility** settings, you can see the **Publish** settings. With a new post, the default is "Immediately." So once the post is published, it will go live on the site immediately. But you can click that **Immediately** link to get another option:

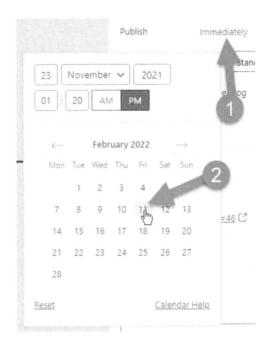

This popup calendar allows you to schedule the post's publication to a future date. Select a date and time in the future to schedule the post, and when that date and time arrives, the post will be automatically published by WordPress.

If you do select a future date and time, the **Publish** button at the top will change to **Schedule.**

Click it, and you'll be asked to confirm everything is correct:

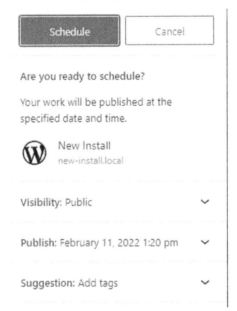

This screen offers a summary of the post and possibly suggestions as well. You can see the visibility and date to be published. In my case, it also suggests I add tags. If everything looks OK, click on the **Schedule** button.

The post will then be published at the selected date and time.

In your **All Posts** screen, scheduled posts are given a "Scheduled" label, and you can see the date they are scheduled for:

You'll also spot that new filter link at the top ;)

Using the HTML Editor to Edit Your Post

There may be times when you want to edit your post in raw HTML code. To do this, click on the **Options** menu button, top right of the Gutenberg editor:

Currently, the **Visual Editor** is selected. It's what we have been using so far. If you choose **Code Editor** instead, you can view/edit the entire post as HTML code.

```
Hello world!

<!-- wp:paragraph -->

<p>Welcome to WordPress. This is your first post. Edit or

delete it, then start writing!</p>

<!-- /wp:paragraph -->
```

You can make changes in the HTML editor and save changes as required. You can revert back to the **Visual Editor** at any time by clicking that item in the same menu.

Editing Posts

At some point after writing a post, you may want to go in and edit or update it. This is an easy process. Just click on **All Posts** in the **Posts** menu. It will open a screen with a list of posts on your site.

Just click on the title of the post you want to edit, and it will open in the editor.

What if you had a lot of posts and needed to find one?

There are two ways of doing this. One is from within your Dashboard using the available search and filtering tools. The other method is one I'll show you later and involves visiting your site while you are logged into the Dashboard.

For now, let's look at three ways we can find posts from within the Dashboard.

Method 1: Perhaps the easiest way of all is to use the **Search Posts** feature. Type in a keyword phrase you know is in the title, and then click the **Search Posts** button.

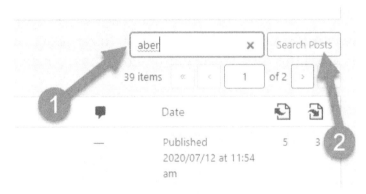

The results will show only those posts that match:

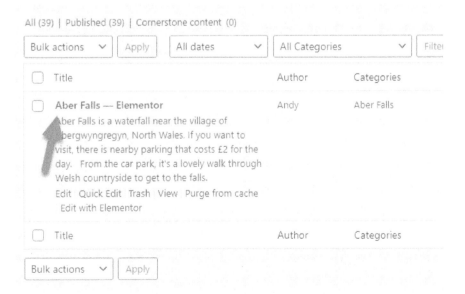

Method 2: If you know what month you wrote the post, you could show all posts from that month by selecting the month from the **All Dates** drop-down box.

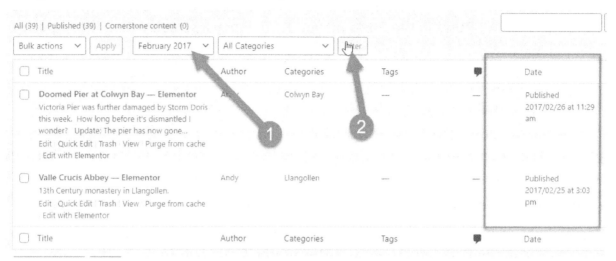

Once selected, click the **Filter** button.

Method 3: You can also search for a post by showing just those posts within a certain category. Select the desired category from the **All Category** drop-down box. Once selected, click the **Filter** button.

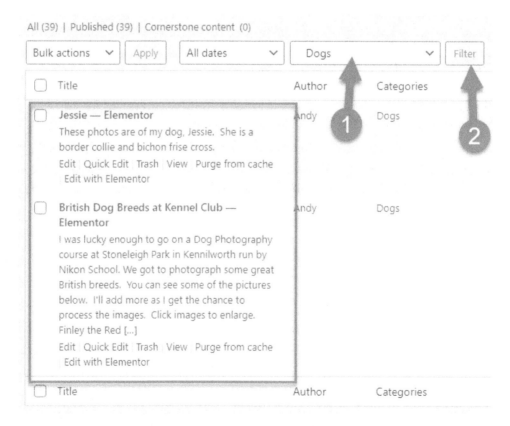

Revisions

Whenever you make changes to a post, WordPress keeps a record (archive) of those changes. You'll see the revisions section in the document properties (as long as you have made changes to the page over time and saved those changes):

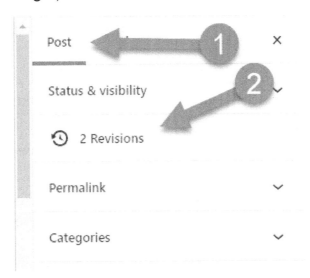

Click on the Revisions section to open it out:

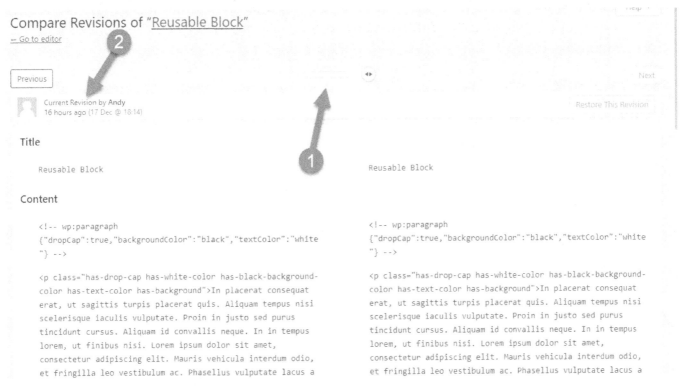

The slider at the top allows you to scroll between the various revisions. As you move through the revisions, you'll see the date and time that revision was saved.

In the main window, you'll see differences between the two revisions highlighted.

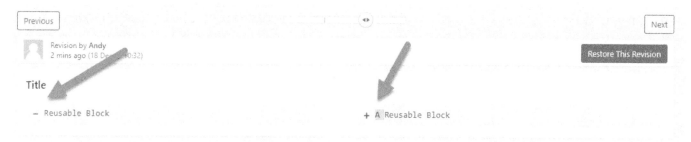

In the above example, I change the title from Reusable Block to A Reusable Block.

The latest version is on the right, and the previous version is on the left. As you scroll back through revisions, you'll always see two versions. On the right will be the version that was saved on that date. On the left was the previous version.

At any time, if you want to revert to a previous version, click the **Restore This Revision** button. The version on the right of the revisions screen will be the one restored. At the same time, a new revision is created for the "latest" version of the post.

Why Use Revisions?

Suppose you are working on a post and delete a paragraph or change an image. Later, you ask yourself, "why did I delete that?" With revisions, you can revert to previous versions of your post with a few mouse clicks.

Tasks to Complete

1. Create a simple post with the title **Dog** and publish it.

2. Change the title to **The Dog** and update.

3. Change the title to **A Dog** and add a paragraph of content to the post. Update again.

4. Open the revisions and move the slider all the way to the left. You can see that the first revision adds the title. Move the slider one spot to the right. This revision shows you updated the title to The Dog. Move the slider to the right one more position. Now you can see this revision changed the title and added a paragraph of content.

5. Play around with these revisions and the **Restore This Revision** until you are happy with how it works.

Differences with Pages

As we discussed earlier, pages are different from posts. On the Add/Edit Page screen, it all looks very similar, but there are a few notable omissions – namely no categories or tags! There is also no box to add an excerpt.

We do, however, have settings for pages that are not found in posts – Page Attributes:

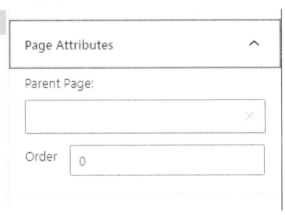

These settings allow you to set up parent-child relationships between your pages. It's not something that most beginners will need, so I won't cover that in this book.

Tasks to Complete

1. Go and look at the page edit screen. Note the page attributes box.

Making it Easy for Visitors to Socially Share Your Content

Having great content on your site is one thing, but getting people to see it is something else.

One of the ways people find a website is through search engines. If we rank well enough for a particular search term, the web searcher may land on our page.

Another way people can find our content is via social media channels. Places like Facebook and Twitter are good examples. To make this more likely, we need to install a social sharing plugin on the site. A social sharing plugin will add buttons to the website that allow people to share the content they are reading with their followers. Social sharing buttons make sharing easy, and therefore more likely.

There are several good social sharing plugins, and I do recommend you look around to find one that matches the design of your website. However, to get you started, let's install my current favorite.

Go to **Add New** in the **Plugins** menu. Search for **Grow Social** by Mediavine and look for this one:

Install and activate the plugin.

You'll see a new menu in the left sidebar labeled **Grow**. Click it.

This plugin offers you two options for displaying social sharing buttons – a floating panel, or embedded in your content.

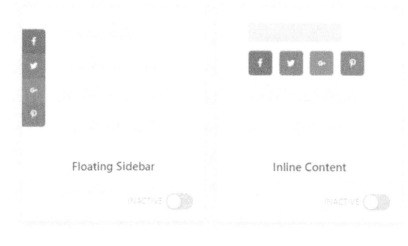

You can use one system or both. To activate a system, click the slider at the bottom. When you do that, a **Settings** button appears:

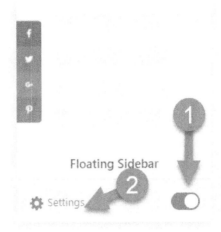

The floating sidebar will create a panel on your web page, which "floats" down the side of your content and is always visible. The inline content option will insert the buttons before and/or after the article on your web page.

Before the social sharing buttons appear on your site, you need to tell the plugin which social accounts you want to include. Click on the settings button.

You can now click the **Select Networks** button to choose which networks you want to work with.

Click on the **Select Networks** button to access the choices.

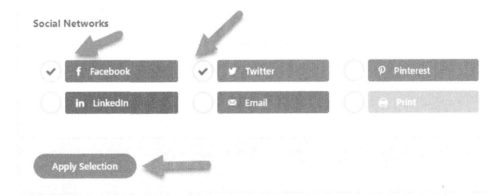

Click the **Apply Selection** button.

The networks will now appear on the settings screen, and you can re-order these by dragging them up or down using the "handle" on the left. You can also delete a network by clicking the "X Remove" link on the right or change the button's label.

Below you'll see some display settings. I'll leave you to explore these options.

When you are ready, scroll to the bottom and make sure that **Post** is checked under the **Post type**

display settings. If you want to include sharing buttons on pages, make sure that is checked too.

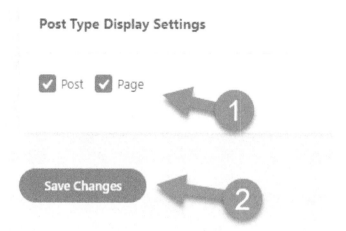

Click **Save Changes.**

If you are using both inline and floating buttons, you need to set them both up separately. You can go back to the main plugin settings by clicking the **Toolkit** link in the sidebar menu.

If you visit your site, you should now see the social sharing buttons on posts (and pages if you enabled that). If you chose floating sidebar, it looks like this:

Notice that the above screenshot is taken while scrolled near the bottom of the post. The social sharing buttons are stuck in position on the left.

If you chose the inline content, it would look like this:

Lorem Ipsum post

Leave a Comment / Uncategorized / By admin

Sharing is caring!

WordPress for Beginners © 1974

This allows people to engage in discussionsThis allows people to engage in discussionsThis allows people to engage in discussionsThis allows people to engage in discussionsThis allows people to engage

Obviously, yours won't look exactly like mine as it depends on the settings you chose. One thing I remove is that **Sharing is caring!** text. You'll find out how to do that in the **Inline Content** settings.

Other Social Share Plugins

Over the years, I have tried lots of social sharing plugins. Some work great, while others only seem to work on some websites and not others. If you find Grow Social does not work properly on *your* site, just search for "social share" in the **Add Plugins** screen and try some.

Tasks to Complete

1. Install a social sharing plugin and set it up to suit your needs.

2. Go to **Add New** in the plugins menu, and search for social sharing plugins to see how many there are. Install some if you want to try them. When finished, uninstall any you are not using.

Internal Linking of Posts

One of the best ways of keeping visitors on your site is to interlink your web pages. There are a few ways of doing this.

The basic way to add a link in your content is to highlight the word or phrase that you want to use as the link's text and then click on the link button in the toolbar.

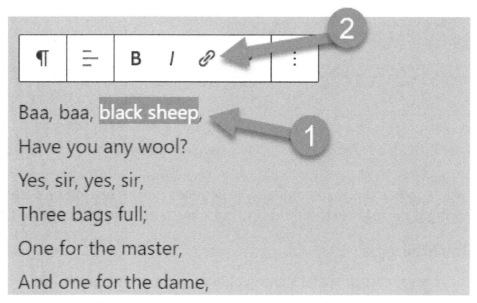

A popup box will appear.

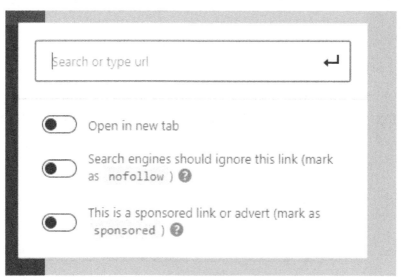

If you want to link to a webpage on a different website, paste the URL into the box.

If you want to link to a post/page on your website, type in part of the title of the webpage, and WordPress will find it for you:

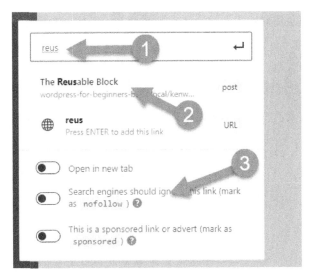

If you want the link to open in a new tab, click the radio button at the bottom to select it. The same goes for the nofollow and sponsored options. When you are happy with your selection, click the post/page in the list that you want to link to. The link will now appear in the post:

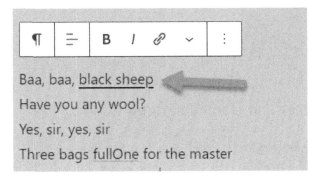

If you need to edit a link you have inserted, click on it to open up this popup:

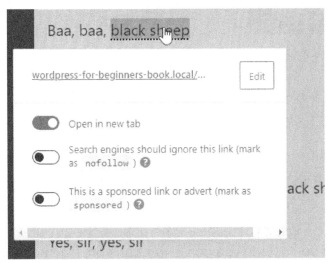

You can now make changes to the URL or the options.

When you have selected a link, if you look at the toolbar at the top, the link icon has changed.

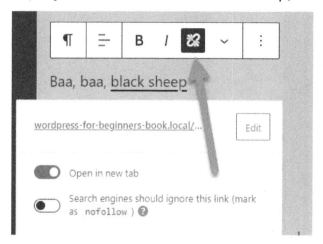

It is now an "unlink" button, which you can use to remove the hyperlink if you want to.

OK, that's the 100% manual way of interlinking your web pages.

Related Posts With YARPP

One way I recommend you inter-link your content is with a plugin called **Yet Another Related Posts**. This plugin allows you to set up a "Related Articles" section at the end of your posts. This will automatically create links to related articles on your site.

Go to the **Add New** Plugin screen and search for **yarpp**.

Install and activate the plugin.

You will now find the **YARPP** menu inside the main **Settings** menu. Click on **YARPP** so we can set this up.

At the top of the YARPP settings is "The Pool." The pool is the set of posts YARPP will use to build a related articles section. If you decide you don't want any posts from a particular category showing up in related article sections, you can exclude that category here by checking the box next to that category. You can do the same by Tag.

There is also an option to limit the age of posts in the pool, only including posts from the previous X days, weeks, or months.

I am going to leave the pool defaults as they are.

If you think you won't be changing these settings, you can hide "The Pool" by unchecking the option in the **Screen Options.**

The next settings on the page are **The Algorithm.** This defines how closely related an article needs to be, to be shown as a "related post."

I recommend you leave the relatedness options with their default values for now. The only change I make on smaller sites is to reduce the Match Threshold, sometimes to a 1 (this value may be your default anyway). However, you can play with this when you have some posts on your site to make sure you are getting suggestions that are related to each post.

Next up are the **Automatic Display Options.**

There is plenty of scope for playing around here as well, including using your own template, but we are going to use the default settings, with one exception. Place a checkmark next to **Show excerpt?** This will give our related posts a description. When you check that box, a few more options appear. Change **Excerpt length** to 50 (I recommend that you experiment with this setting).

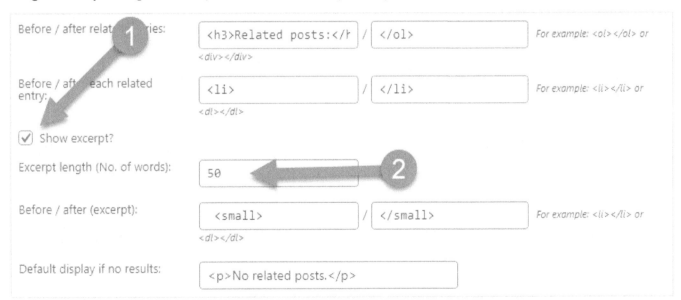

Ok, that is all we are changing. Scroll to the bottom and click **Save Changes.**

You will now have a related posts section at the end of every post on the site. You probably won't see much yet because you don't have content on the site. Here is what I see at the end of my post on this demo site:

And one for the dame

One for the little boy

Who lives down the laneBaa, baa, black sheep

Have you any wool?

Yes, sir, yes, sir

Three bags full

No related posts.

However, as you start adding content, the related posts section will start to populate with recommendations for your visitors. If it doesn't, then play around with the **Match Threshold** in **The Algorithm** settings. Reducing it should result in more matches.

Here is an example of a related posts section on one of my sites using this plugin.

Related Posts

1. What Is an Attachment in WordPress?

   WordPress posts and pages can contain attachments. They include images, videos, podcasts, and various documents, etc. Used correctly, attachments enhance the visitor experience and improve SE rankings.

2. What Is A Shortcode in WordPress?

   Learn about WordPress shortcode and how it puts the power of coding into the hands of every site owner. No Skills Needed! It's a fast, immediate, and cool way to add dynamic website features.

3. What Is a WordPress Favicon and How to Create One?

   Read this quick quite on the 3 ways to create and install a custom favicon in WordPress. Websites with favicons look more professional, enhance the site's reputation, and have higher trust levels.

This "related posts" section was on an article about WordPress on my ezSEONews.com site. Can you see the benefits? People who are reading the main WordPress article are shown other articles that are related to what they've just been reading about. It gives us another chance to keep the visitor on our site.

We have looked at two ways we can inter-link our content.

Firstly, we can manually create links in the content. Secondly, we can use a plugin like YARPP to show related posts to our visitors.

The last option I like to use is a plugin that I can set up to control internal linking on an automated basis but without losing control over the linking.

I have written an article on internal site linking using a plugin. If you are interested, you should read that article here:

https://ezseonews.com/backlinks/internal-linking-seo/

The plugin I mention in that article is not free. If you want to try this on your own site and want a free plugin, check out **Internal Link Juicer** or **Internal Links Manager**.

Tasks to Complete

1. Go and edit an existing post or create one for this exercise. Manually add a few links on this page. They can be links to pages on your site or another website entirely.

2. Open the page in a web browser and check that the links you added work properly.

3. Install YARPP and configure it. As you add more content to your website, check out the related posts section (found at the end of every post).

4. Read the article on automated internal linking and try it yourself with one of the free plugins.

The Homepage of Your Site - Blog or Static?

WordPress is a tool that was originally created as a blogging platform (publishing date-related content as posts). The way in which WordPress handles these posts by default is to post them on the homepage, with the latest post at the top of that page.

In the settings, we saw that we could define how many posts to include on a page with the default set at 10. That means the last ten posts published on the site will show up on the homepage in chronological order, with the latest post at the top and older posts below. As you post more content on the site, the older posts scroll off the bottom of the homepage and are replaced by the newer ones at the top.

If that is the type of site you want, then that's fine. You can ignore this section and leave things at their default settings.

Personally, I like to create a homepage that always displays the content I want my visitors to see on the homepage. In fact, I create a "homepage article" describing the main point of the site and helping visitors with navigation.

The good news is that creating this type of "static" homepage in WordPress is easy.

Create a WordPress "page" (not a post) and write your homepage content. Give the page a real title. Don't just call it "Homepage" as some themes (though not Twenty Twenty-One) will show this title at the top of your homepage.

For this demo, I've called mine **Amateur Radio News**. Once completed, make sure you publish it. You cannot set up a static homepage with a draft page.

Go to the **Reading** settings inside the **Settings** menu.

At the top of the screen, you'll see a section called **Your Homepage Displays,** and there are two radio buttons:

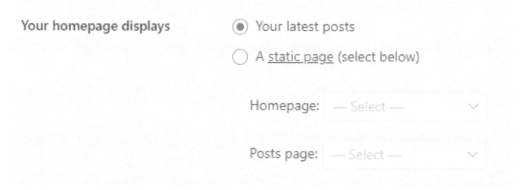

As we've said before, the default setting for your homepage is to display your latest posts. You can see that it is selected. However, we can use the WordPress page we created a moment ago by choosing **A Static Page**. When you do that, the two drop-down boxes become activated.

The top one labeled **Homepage** is the one we are interested in. Click on the drop-down box and select the page you created with your homepage article.

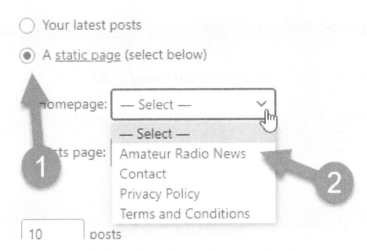

At the bottom of your page, click on the **Save Changes** button.

OK, you are all set. Go to your homepage, and you'll see the article you selected is now your homepage.

You can see how easy it is to create this type of static page for the homepage of your website.

No matter how many posts you add to your site, that homepage "article" will not change (unless you change it).

OK, I hear your question.

"If the homepage just shows the same article, how are people going to find all my other web pages?"

Well, that's where the website navigation system comes in. We'll look at that next.

Tasks to Complete

1. If you want your homepage to show the same article, create a WordPress page with that article. Edit the **Reading** settings to show that page on your **Homepage**.

Navigation Menus

To add or edit a navigation menu in WordPress, go to **Menus** inside the **Appearance** menu.

Let's design a menu for our website. In it, we'll add links to the legal pages we created – Contact, Privacy Policy, and Terms.

Add a name in the **Menu Name** box, and click the **Create Menu** button:

Menu structure

Menu Name | Legal Menu | ← ①

Give your menu a name, then click Create Menu.

Menu Settings

Auto add pages ☐ Automatically add new top-level pages to this menu

Display location ☐ Primary menu
☐ Secondary menu

② → **Create Menu**

I've called my menu "Legal Menu" to reflect its purpose. This makes things easier when you have multiple menus, and you are trying to decide which one is which.

On the left of the screen, you'll have a section that lists all Pages, Posts, Custom Links, Categories & Tags. Pull down the **Screen Options** and check Tags if it is not there.

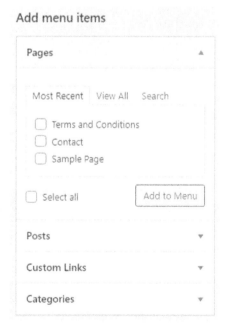

You can now add any post, page, category page, or tag page to the menu.

Currently, the Pages section is expanded. You can see three tabs at the top: **Most Recent, View All,** and **Search.** These will help you find a specific page so that you can insert it into the menu.

To expand a different section, click on the section.

Try it. Click on **Posts,** and you'll see it open as the **Pages** section collapse.

Since we want to add legal pages, click on the **Pages** section to expand it. We want the privacy policy, terms, and contact. If you can see them all on the **Most Recent** screen, check the box next to each one. If you don't see them all listed in **Most Recent**, click on **View All** tab, and you will find them there.

With all three checked, click the **Add to Menu** button,

You will see all three added to the menu on the right-hand side of the screen:

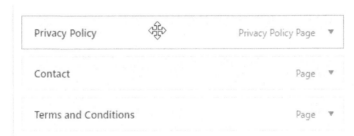

If you move your mouse over one of the items in the menu, the cursor changes:

This cursor indicates that the item can be dragged and dropped. Click and drag it up or down to re-order the items in the menu. I want Terms at the top, then privacy, and contact at the bottom.

You'll also notice some settings at the bottom of the screen:

The **Auto Add Pages** option will automatically add new pages you create on the site to this menu. That typically isn't something we want, so leave it unchecked.

The second option defines the location of the menu within the theme. The Twenty Twenty-One theme has two locations assigned to menus. One is the primary menu, and the other is the secondary menu.

The Primary menu is across the top of the site, to the right of the header.

The secondary menu is in the footer areas for this theme:

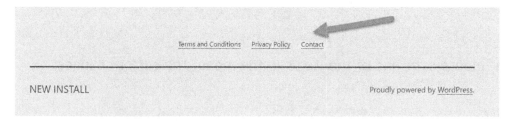

If you are using a different theme and want to know where the menu locations are on the page, add the menu to a location and save. Then visit your site to check.

I'll check **Primary Menu** and **Save**.

Menu Hierarchy

It is possible to create hierarchical drop-down menus. In other words, each item in the menu can have a parent or child type relationship.

To illustrate, I want to create a new custom menu item.

Click on **Custom Links**. Fill it in like this and click **Add to Menu**:

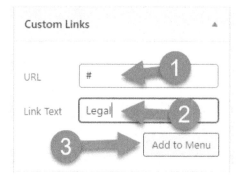

The new **Legal** item will be added to the bottom of the list, so I'll drag it up to the top.

Now you need to drag the Terms, Privacy & Contact menu items over to the right a little to indent them:

And **Save Menu.**

We can see the new menu on my site if I refresh the homepage in my browser:

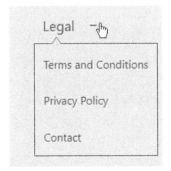

But as soon as I move my mouse cursor over the Legal menu, the rest of the menu pops up:

Clicking any of the items in the sub-menu will take you to those pages. However, click on the word Legal. The page will likely jump up a little. That is because of the # sign we added to the URL box in the custom menu item. The thing is, to create the menu item, you need something in the URL box. However, once it is created, we can delete it.

Go back to the menu and expand the **Legal** custom link:

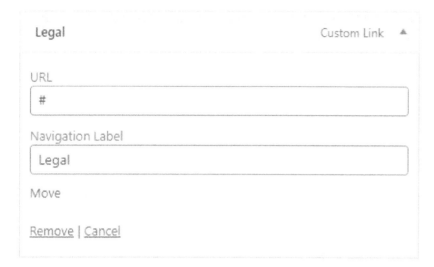

Delete the # and **Save Menu**.

If you go back to check the menu again, the Legal part of the menu is no longer a link, and clicking it makes no difference.

This hierarchy technique can be used to tidy up big menus with lots of items, but it does not make sense to do so in the above example. It's easy enough to fix though, just remove the **Legal** custom link by expanding that item in the menu and clicking the **Remove** link. All the other items will un-indent themselves. Save the menu.

On the **Menus** screen, you'll probably have noticed two tabs at the top – **Edit Menus** and **Manage Locations**. The Edit Menus screen is the one we have been working on to create this menu. The Manage Locations screen is another way to assign the location of the menus. Have a look at that tab and decide if you want to use it. For me, it is just easier using the **Display location** options we've already seen at the bottom of the **Edit Menus** screen.

Other Menu Item Settings

We've already seen that each menu item we add has a little arrow on the far right. We use this to access the settings for that menu item:

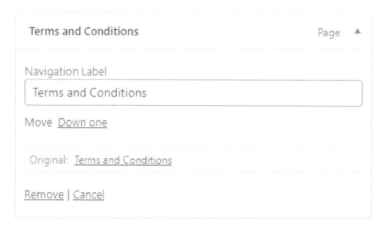

You can edit the **Navigation Label** if you want.

At the bottom, you can see a **Remove** link to delete the menu item.

The default link settings only provide the options shown above, as some are hidden. Open the **Screen Options** and check the options for **Link Target** and **Link Relationship (XFN)**. Now close the screen options and check out the new options:

The **Link target** creates the checkbox so you can choose to have menu links open in a new browser tab.

The **Link Relationship** allows you to add nofollow tags to your links. If you don't know what these are, don't worry. Simply put, the nofollow tag tells a search engine that a page you are linking to is not important. I often use these on links to my legal pages, like this:

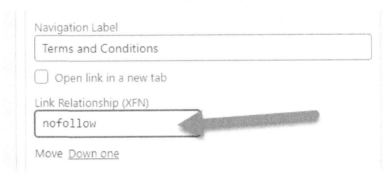

While we are in this menu item, I am going to shorten the Navigation label to just **Terms**. On saving the menu, that change is updated on the site:

Edit an Existing Menu

There will be times when you want to edit an existing menu. This is straightforward enough. Go to **Menus** in the **Appearance** menu.

If you only have one menu, that is the one you will see. If you have more than one menu created, use the drop-down box to choose the menu you want to edit:

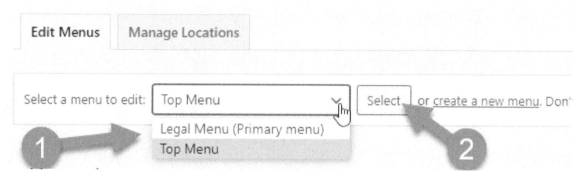

Click the **Select** button to switch to that menu and edit.

Navigation Menu Widgets

Any menu you create can be added to an area that accepts widgets by using the navigation menu widget. You can use a menu you already have or create a new one. I tend to give my menus names that refer to their function or location.

Let's **Create a new menu:**

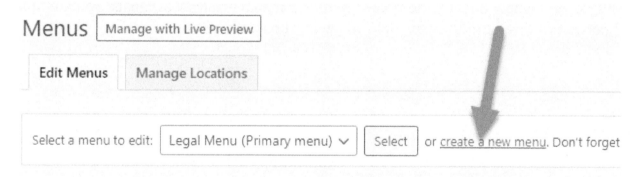

I am calling mine **Footer Menu**. Enter the name and click the **Create Menu** button.

I am only going to add the following to mine:

1. Homepage (found on the Pages tab).

2. Contact Us (Found on the Pages tab).

I'll change the label on my Homepage link from **Amateur Radio News** to **Home** and put that first. After saving, here is my menu:

Menu structure

Menu Name	Footer Menu	

Drag the items into the order you prefer. Click the arrow on the right of the item to reveal ad

☐ Bulk Select

Home	Front Page	▼
Contact	Page	▼

OK, head over to **Widgets** in the **Appearance** menu.

When you get there, add a **Navigation Menu** widget into the **Footer** area:

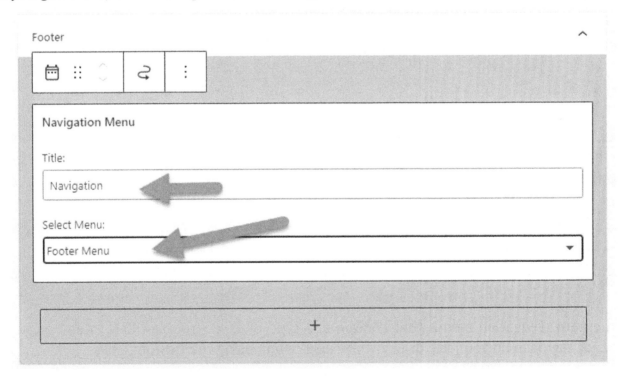

Add a title and select the menu from the drop-down box.

Save the widget by clicking the **Update** button, then check out the footer on your site:

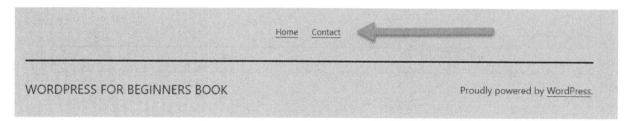

Of course, with the Twenty Twenty-One theme, there is a footer menu location built into the theme, so I didn't need to use a widget. Remember the **Secondary Location**?

Menu Settings

Auto add pages	☐ Automatically add new top-level pages to this menu
Display location	☐ Primary menu (Currently set to: Legal Menu)
	☐ Secondary menu

Delete Menu

However, the display format is different. Above you see the menu created with a navigation menu widget in the footer area. Below you see the same menu used in the footer location built into the theme:

You can create navigation menus that contain any type of link. You can link to any page, post, category, or tag page on your site or anywhere else online using the Custom Links.

Tip: If you wanted to offer your visitors a PDF download, you could use the PDF's URL as a menu item.

The menu system built into WordPress gives you the flexibility you need as you design and develop your website.

Tasks to Complete

1. Go and experiment with Navigation Menus.

2. Create a menu with a "Home" link (custom link to homepage URL) and links to the "legal" pages on your site.

3. Add the menu to all of your theme's built-in locations and see where the menu ends up on the web page.

4. Add the menu to a widgetized area of your site.

Viewing Your Site While Logged In

Something special happens when you are visiting your website while logged into the Dashboard.

Earlier, when we were looking at the User Profile, we made sure an option was checked - **Show Toolbar when viewing site**. Let's see what happens with that option enabled.

Log in to your dashboard and then open your website in another tab of your web browser. What you'll see is a very useful "ribbon" across the top of your website:

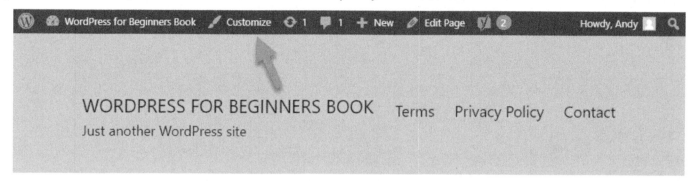

This ribbon gives you access to some important WordPress features. For example, if you want to edit a page or post on your website, you can visit your website, find the post, then click on the edit post link in the ribbon bar. That will open the post in the WordPress Dashboard, ready for editing.

In the screenshot above, I am on the site homepage. You can see a link to **Edit Page**. If I click on that, I am taken into the Gutenberg editor with the homepage loaded up and ready to edit.

The ribbon is very useful as you browse your site. If you find errors on a web page, just click the **Edit Page/Post** link, fix the issue(s), and then click the **Update** button.

Some items in the menu have drop-down options. Mouseover your site name on the left, and you'll have links to:

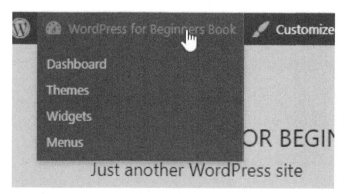

These links will take you directly to those areas of the Dashboard. There is also a quick way to add new content to your site. Mouseover the **+ New** item to quickly add a new post, page, media item, or user:

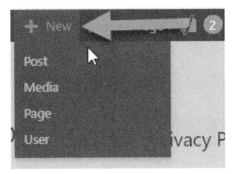

There is a **Customize** link in the admin bar that takes you directly to the Customize screen in the Dashboard.

If you installed the Yoast SEO plugin, that adds a drop-down menu to the toolbar, too, offering quick SEO links. I'll leave you to explore those.

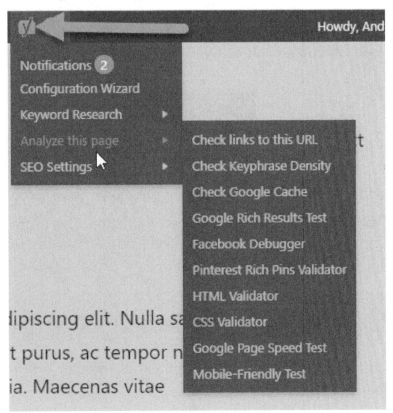

Finally, on the right, if you mouse over your name, you'll get this menu:

These options are self-explanatory.

The ribbon has a couple of useful indicators too. If you have any updates that need installing, the update indicator will tell you:

If you mouse over this, it will tell you what needs updating. In my case, it's one plugin. Clicking the update indicator will take you to the **Update** section of the Dashboard.

There is also a speech bubble that represents comments awaiting moderation. If there are comments waiting, the speech bubble will tell you how many. In my case, I have two comments awaiting moderation:

Clicking the speech bubble will open the Dashboard on the moderation screen.

This admin bar is only visible when you are logged into your site. Therefore, your site visitors will never see it ;)

Tasks to Complete

1. Log in to your site.

2. Open the site in a new tab in your browser.

3. Mouseover, then click every option in the ribbon bar at the top. See what these links do and where they take you when you click them.

WordPress Security

WordPress has often been criticized for being too easy to hack. There have been a lot of cases where people have lost their WordPress site after a hacker gained access to it and wreaked havoc. Several years ago, one of my sites got hacked so badly that I just deleted the whole thing and let the domain expire. At that time, I didn't have a reliable backup system in place.

The good news is that WordPress today is very secure. Any security vulnerabilities that are discovered are fixed quickly and updates issued. Most hacking problems are the fault of the person running the site. My site that was hacked was using a plugin that turned out to be insecure. I hadn't updated it in years, and that goes down as my fault.

In this chapter, I want to go through the measures you can take to protect your site.

We set up a plugin earlier called UpdraftPlus. That is creating backups for us, and it is a great start.

Another layer of protection is always to **upgrade WordPress** as soon as there is a new update available. The WordPress team fix security leaks as soon as they are found. Therefore, if your Dashboard says there is a WordPress upgrade, install it as soon as possible to make sure your copy has all the bug fixes and/or security patches.

Always update plugins when updates are available.

Uninstall any theme you are not using, and always keep your active theme up to date.

Finally, I'd recommend you install the All-in-One Security plugin. I install it on all my own sites. The plugin is complex and beyond the scope of this book, but I did record a video tutorial to get you started:

https://ezseonews.com/blog/all-in-one-wp-security-firewall/

If that URL is too long to type, visit https://ezseonews.com and search for **Security**.

For those that want more guidance on security, I have a full video course on the topic of WordPress Security and how to make sure your site is virtually hack-proof. If you want more details on that, please see my courses in the resources at the end of the book.

Tasks to Complete

1. Make sure UpdraftPlus is making regular backups of your site and preferably storing them in the cloud, e.g., on Dropbox.

2. Always keep WordPress (and plugins) up to date.

3. Always update plugins.

4. Uninstall any theme you are not using.

5. Watch the free All in One Security Firewall video from the link above and consider setting it up to secure your website.

Monitoring Website Traffic

Every Webmaster wants to know how many visitors their site is getting and how those people are finding their pages (search engines, social media channels, etc.).

Fortunately, there are good (and free) solutions to give you this information.

The tool I use on my own sites is called **Google Analytics**, but it is complex and perhaps overkill for someone just starting out. I'd, therefore, recommend you check out a free service like "Get Clicky":

http://clicky.com/

I won't go into details on setting this up, but it is straightforward. You'll need to sign up for a free account and then install tracking on your website. This plugin can help and was created by the same team that brought us Yoast SEO:

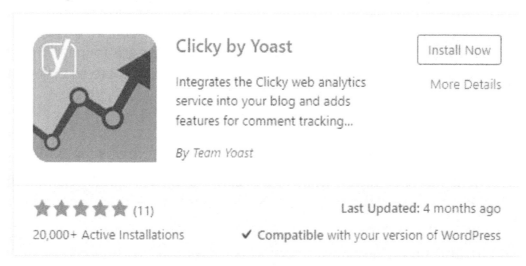

Once integrated into your site, Clicky will monitor your visitors. You'll get information about where they come from and what they do on your site.

As your site grows, I'd highly recommend you investigate Google Analytics and make the switch. It's the best free tool out there and gives a wealth of information about your visitors.

Tasks to Complete

1. Install web analytics on your site. Sign up for **Clicky**.

2. Install the "Clicky by Yoast" plugin and configure it as per the installation instructions on the plugin site.

3. Log in to your Get Clicky account and explore the reports and options. Use their help if needed.

4. When you have time, investigate Google Analytics.

Building the 3 Site Models

Earlier in the book, we looked at three different site structures using posts and pages. These were the business site, blog, and hybrid site.

In this chapter, I want to revisit these three models and cover the steps required to create each one. I won't be going into much detail with the steps because the "how-to" has already been covered. e.g., I may say, "create a Page." You know how to do that, so there is no need for more instruction than that. However, after we look at each model, I will give you a link to a video I created showing the process of building that type of site.

I'll start by reminding you of the three site structures.

A Business Site

A business site typically uses WordPress Pages for the main site content, rather than posts. However, it is common for business sites also to include a blog, where the business can make announcements. Here is that site structure:

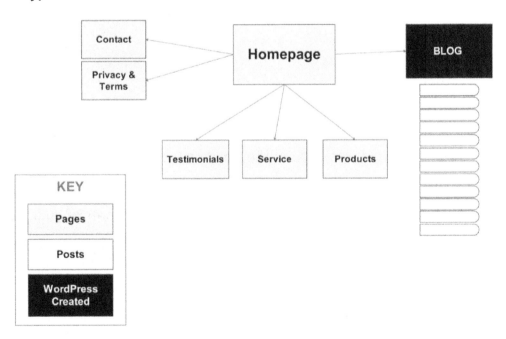

Before we look at the steps to create this type of site structure, I need to introduce you to a new concept that works nicely on Business style sites when you need to set up a blog.

The Posts Page

One feature you may find useful in WordPress is the ability to create a "Posts Page." The posts page does what its name suggests - displays all of the WordPress posts on this page.

This feature is most useful for a business type site, where most of the site is built with Pages, but you want to have a blog, e.g., for company announcements.

Creating a Posts Page

1. Create a new blank page and publish it. I'll call mine, "Blog."
2. Go to the reading settings, and set the **Posts page** to the blank page you just created:
3. Save the settings.

Visit the page, and you'll see that all posts on the site are now listed on this "posts page."

OK, we have enough to continue.

Steps to Create this Business Site

1. Create the Contact, Terms, and Privacy pages.

2. Create the Homepage.

3. Create the following business pages: Testimonials, Services & Products.

4. Create a blank Blog page.

5. Assign the Blog page you created to the Posts Page in the Reading Settings.

6. Write some blog posts.

7. Create a Legal Menu with contact, privacy & Terms, and insert it into the footer of your site.

8. Create a Top Menu with Testimonials, Services, Products & Blog pages included. Insert the menu into the header of the site.

To watch a typical business structure being built, watch this video:

https://ezseonews.com/wp4b-tutorials/#business

A Blog

A typical blog is based on WordPress posts to create an organized, chronological sequence of web pages. The homepage of a blog is typically just a list of all the posts in chronological order. However, you can also create a blog-style site that has a static homepage. WordPress pages will only be used for contact, privacy, etc. Here is that structure:

A Typical Blog

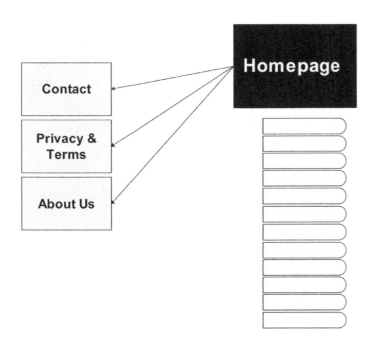

Steps to Create this Blog Site

1. Create Contact, Privacy, Terms, and About Us as WordPress pages.

2. Create a Legal menu, including links to Contact, Privacy, Terms, and About Us.

3. Add the menu to the top of your website.

4. Write some blog posts. These will appear on your homepage.

5. Alternatively, you can create a static homepage and a Blog page. You would then need a menu to direct visitors to the blog.

To watch a typical blog structure being built, watch this video:

https://ezseonews.com/wp4b-tutorials/#blog

A Hybrid Website (Typical Site)

The typical WordPress website has a static homepage and a number of posts, organized into categories. There will be a few WordPress pages for contact, privacy, etc. The site may or may not have a separate blog. Here is that structure:

WordPress "Hybrid"

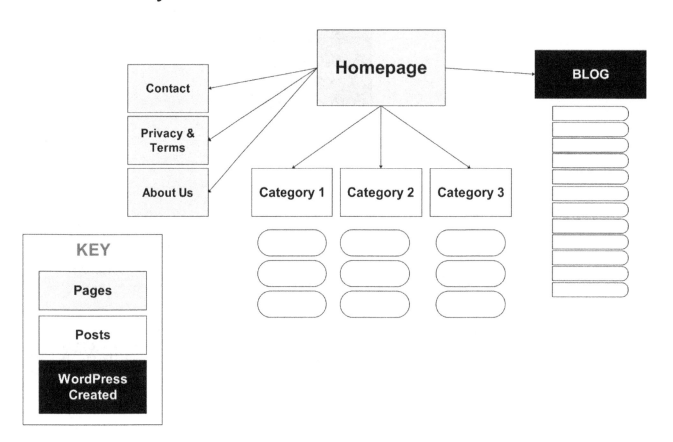

Steps to Create this Hybrid Site

1. Create Contact, Privacy, Terms & About Us as pages.

2. Create a page to be used as your homepage.

3. In Writing Settings, change the settings to show your static homepage on the homepage of your site.

4. Create categories for all content you want to include on your site, and start writing posts in each of those categories.

5. Create a special **Blog** category that you can use for a separate blog.

6. Start writing some blog posts.

7. Create a legal menu including Contact, Privacy, and Terms and place this menu in your site's footer.

8. Create a menu containing your categories and put that menu in the most appropriate place. If your site has a sidebar, that would be a good place. You also need to have a link to your blog somewhere, so put that in the same menu, or perhaps a **Top Menu** that also includes a link **Home**.

To watch a typical Hybrid structure being built, watch this video:

https://ezseonews.com/wp4b-tutorials/#hybrid

Appendix I. Search Engine Optimization (SEO)

Search Engine Optimization has changed a lot in the last few years. It has always been one of the most important aspects of building a website because it helps you to rank better in Google, and consequently get more traffic, and make more sales from your pages.

Today, things are very different. If you overdo your optimization, Google is likely to penalize you and dump your site out of its search engine.

If you ask Google about the best way to optimize your site, it would probably tell you to avoid Search Engine Optimization altogether, focus on visitor experience, and not worry about search engines.

Despite sounding like a lost cause, you should still consider a number of "best practices" as you build your website. I will list the main things to consider here, but if you want a more in-depth discussion about SEO, I'd highly recommend my own book on the subject called **SEO 2021 & Beyond - Search Engine Optimization will never be the same again.**

Main Points for Safe SEO

1. Always write content for the visitor, not the search engines.

2. Always create the highest quality content possible and make it unique. More than that, add something to your content that is not found on any other websites covering the same or similar topic. Use your personal voice, experiences, and thoughts.

3. Engage your visitor and allow them to open discussions with you through the built-in comment feature.

4. Never try to write content based on keyword phrases. Always write content on a topic. E.g., don't write an article on "best iPhone case," write an article on "Which iPhone Case offers the best protection for your phone?" See the difference?

5. As a measure of whether your content is good enough, ask yourself if you could imagine your article appearing in a glossy magazine? If you answer no, then it's not good enough to publish on your own website.

6. DO NOT hire people to build backlinks to your site. If you want to build some links, they need to be on high-quality web pages. You can find more specific advice in my SEO book.

7. Add a social sharing plugin to your site so that people can quickly share your content on social channels like Facebook, Twitter, YouTube, and Instagram, etc.

The best advice I can give you for present-day SEO is to **read and digest Google's Webmaster Guidelines**. They are there to help us create sites that will rank well in their Search Engine Results Pages, aka SERPs. You can read those guidelines here:

https://ezseonews.com/wmg

Tasks to Complete

1. Read Google's Webmaster Guidelines repeatedly until you know them off by heart. They really are very important and will benefit you in the long run; providing you adhere to their suggestions, of course

Where to Go from Here?

We've covered a lot of ground in this book. You should now be confident in finding your way around the WordPress Dashboard.

You have installed WordPress, installed the essential plugins, and configured everything so that your site is now ready for content.

So, what's the next step?

Create impressive content!

Create content, publish & repeat.

I have a couple of resources you may find useful.

YouTube Channel

Lots of video tutorials on using WordPress.

http://ezseonews.com/yt

O.M.G. Facebook Group

A group I initially created for my course students, but I welcome book readers too! Meet, chat, and discuss with other WordPress users. This is an ad-free zone, so you won't be bombarded with people trying to sell you stuff. You will be asked where you heard about the group when you click join, so just say you are a reader of the book.

http://ezseonews.com/omg

My Site

Find lots of Wordpress tutorials. You can sign up for my newsletter while you are there to get notified of new tutorials, books, courses, etc.

https://ezseonews.com/

Useful Resources

There are a few places that I would recommend you visit for more information.

WordPress Tutorials on my Website

https://ezseonews.com/category/wordpress/

My Other Webmaster Books

All my books are available as Kindle books and paperbacks. You can view them all here:

https://amazon.com/author/drandrewwilliams

I'll leave you to explore those if you are interested. You'll find books on various aspects of being a webmaster, such as creating high-quality content, SEO, CSS, etc.

My Video Courses

I have a growing number of video courses hosted on Udemy. You can view a complete list of these at my site:

https://ezseonews.com/udemy

There are courses on the same kinds of topics that my books cover, so SEO, Content Creation, WordPress, Website Analytics, etc.

Google Webmaster Guidelines

https://ezseonews.com/wmg – this is the webmaster's bible of what is acceptable and what is not in the eyes of the world's biggest search engine.

Google Analytics

http://www.google.com/analytics/ – the best free analytics program out there. When you have some free time to learn how to use Google Analytics, I recommend you upgrade from Get Clicky.

WordPress Glossary

This glossary lists some of the technical terms I've used in this book. You may also hear these terms when watching other videos or tutorials online. Don't let this list scare you. You do not need to know all of these. This list is for reference only. As you go through this book, if you hear a word you don't understand, look here.

Administrator / Admin - The person that is responsible for maintaining the website, adding pages, etc.

Category Silo - A silo is a closely related group of posts that link to each other, but not to less related posts. For example, you might have a category on your site about mountain bikes. All posts in that category are about mountain bikes and link to other articles on mountain bikes. Categories in WordPress allow you to group posts into these silos, so you might hear the term category silo, simply meaning a group of highly related posts, all in the same category.

cPanel - This is your web host control panel that provides an easy to use interface and automation tools to simplify your job as site admin.

Child Theme - This is a WordPress theme that inherits its functionality from a parent theme. The parent theme needs to be installed as well as the child theme. Changes made to the child theme won't affect the parent theme so that you can update the parent theme as and when updates are available, without trashing your site.

CSS - The layout and design of a web page and its contents are controlled by CSS. This stands for Cascading Style Sheets. You can change colors, font size, alignment of text or images, etc., all using CSS.

Database - A database is a file that contains information. WordPress stores your site content and settings in the database.

Dashboard - This is the WordPress control panel, where you log in to add/edit your website.

Directory (or folder) - You organize files on your computer into folders (also called directories). Web Servers are just computers, and files are organized into directories (or folders) on servers as well.

DNS - DNS stands for Domain Name System. It's a system that converts domain names into numeric IP addresses. See also, Registrar and web host.

Domain / Domain Name - This is your website's web address. e.g., mydomain.com

FTP - Stands for File Transfer Protocol. This is a system for connecting to your webspace so you can add, edit, delete files, etc. Using a tool called an FTP client, you can view all files and folders on your server in much the same way you can with a File Explorer on your computer.

.htaccess - This is a file that is processed by your web server before your web page is loaded in a web browser. You can add specific messages to this file, e.g., to prevent certain people from accessing your site or redirecting an old URL to a new URL.

Host - See Web Host

HTTPS - HTTP defines how content is formatted and transmitted around the web as well as how web servers react to that content. HTTPS is the same as HTTP but uses SSL to ensure content is encrypted.

IP address - This is a unique string of numbers and full stops (periods) that uniquely identify a computer on the internet.

MySQL - This is an open-source database that is commonly used with WordPress installations as well as other web applications.

Plugins - Plugins are pieces of software that can "plugin" to WordPress to add new features. e.g., a plugin might allow you to create a contact form or backup your database on a schedule.

Protocol - Essentially, a set of rules that define how something works.

Registrar - Also called the domain registrar. This is the company that registers your domain for you. They will renew it if you want to. When someone comes to your website, the registrar will send them to your web host via the DNS settings at the registrar. Each web host has a unique DNS, so the visitor will be sent to your web host, where your WordPress site is installed.

Responsive Theme - These themes adjust to the size of the web browser. If someone is viewing your site on a mobile phone, the responsive theme makes sure it looks great. The same site in a desktop browser will also look great as the responsive theme adjusts the layout accordingly.

Root folder - This is the top-level folder on your server where a website is installed. On your home computer, the root folder for any application you have installed will be the folder that contains all the files and sub-folders for that application.

RSS Feed - Stands for Rich Site Summary or Really Simple Syndication. It is a file that contains details of the last X posts on your website. Each post will have details of title, date, description, etc.

SEO - Stands for Search Engine Optimization and refers to the methods you use to try to get your site to rank higher in the search engines.

Shortcodes - A WordPress specific code that you can use to insert something into a website. E.g., a contact form plugin may give you a shortcode like [cf-form-1]. When the page is rendered in the browser, the shortcode is replaced by the contact form.

SSL - Stands for Secure Sockets Layer. It's a security measure to ensure a connection between two computers is encrypted.

Themes - These are the "skins" of your site. They control the fonts, colors & layout of your site. You can change the look and feel of your site by changing the theme. It takes seconds to do.

URL - the web address you type into your web browser.

Web Host - This is the company that rents you disk space on their computers (servers). You can use that disk space to install your website. When someone visits your website, it's delivered from that web host. The web host has a unique DNS that you give to your registrar.

Webmaster - Same as administrator.

wp-config.php - This file contains the basic setup information for your WordPress site, like database name and other database settings.

Widgets - These are plug and play pieces of software that can add features to various areas of your website. e.g., there is a widget that displays a calendar, and this could be placed in the sidebar.

Please Leave a Review/Thought on Amazon

If you enjoyed this book, or even if you didn't, I'd love to hear your comments about it. You can leave your thoughts on the Amazon website.

Index

Made in the USA
Coppell, TX
13 October 2022